D1132002

TWAYNE'S WORLD AUTHORS SERIES

A Survey of the World's Literature

Sylvia E. Bowman, Indiana University

GENERAL EDITOR

SOVIET UNION

N. P. Vaslef, U.S. Air Force Academy

EDITOR

Anna Akhmatova

(TWAS 198)

TWAYNE'S WORLD AUTHORS SERIES (TWAS)

The purpose of TWAS is to survey the major writers —novelists, dramatists, historians, poets, philosophers, and critics—of the nations of the world. Among the national literatures covered are those of Australia, Canada, China, Eastern Europe, France, Germany, Greece, India, Italy, Japan, Latin America, the Netherlands, New Zealand, Poland, Russia, Scandinavia, Spain, and the African nations, as well as Hebrew, Yiddish, and Latin Classical literatures. This survey is complemented by Twayne's United States Authors Series and English Authors Series.

The intent of each volume in these series is to present a critical-analytical study of the works of the writer; to include biographical and historical material that may be necessary for understanding, appreciation, and critical appraisal of the writer; and to present all material in clear, concise English—but not to vitiate the scholarly content of the work by doing so.

Anna Akhmatova

SAM N. DRIVER
Brown University

Twayne Publishers, Inc.   : :   New York

Preface

Anna Akhmatova (1889–1966) is one of the most arresting figures in modern Russian poetry. Her extraordinary literary career and her tragic personal life made Akhmatova a legend within her own lifetime. An established poet before the First World War, Akhmatova created a lyric poetry which has been much admired for its technical accomplishment and economy of expression. Her art matured through the years of the October Revolution and the Civil War. In the dark decades that followed, Akhmatova steadfastly refused to compromise her artistic integrity, despite official pressures and persecutions which were at times almost intolerable. Except for a brief period during the Second World War, her original poetry was not published until 1956. As the works which were written during her long period of silence began to appear in print, it became clear that Akhmatova had undergone an amazing growth and development. Although essentially consistent with her mature style of the twenties, her poetry had moved from predominantly love lyrics to broader themes, at times almost epic. She wrote of a Russia that once had been and of a Russia that was. She wrote of the past in the present, as the last link between a great age of Russian poetry and the present day. She had become not only the *grande dame* of Russian letters, but because of her refusal to accept literary regimentation, the very symbol of uncompromising artistic integrity.

The main emphasis of this study of Akhmatova's poetry is on the formative decade, 1912–1922. First of all, this significant period in Akhmatova's career has been insufficiently studied. Apart from two books and a number of interesting articles published in the 1920's,* there have been no scholarly studies of Akhmatova's work in the Soviet Union until the very recent past. Further, Akhmatova remains a highly controversial figure in the Soviet Union, and there is no reason to expect a truly objective assessment by Soviet scholars for some time to come. Her past intransigeance and recent outspokenness in regard to artistic integrity would seem to preclude,

---

* List included in Bibliography.

for the time being at least, such a treatment. There have been only very limited studies of Akhmatova in the West.

A second reason for the emphasis on the early period is that we have a clear image of Akhmatova and observe complete continuity in her work only up through the early 1920's. For the two decades following, the image of both the poet and the person is obscure. Rumors concerning Akhmatova's life during these years are often contradictory and seem of doubtful validity; most of the biographical sources which are available have been rejected *in toto* by Akhmatova herself as "unreliable." The poems written during this period and published later can scarcely be entirely representative of the whole production of the time. Those poems and fragments which have most recently appeared are intriguing, but it would be difficult to study them without reference to the larger body of poetry. Although there is now in progress a collection of Akhmatova's works, one may expect that a truly complete collection will not appear for some time.[1]

For these reasons, this study concentrates primarily on the period 1912–1922. The lyric poetry of these is represented by five volumes: *Evening (Vecher)* (1912), *Rosary (Chyotki)* (1914), *The White Flock (Belaya staya)* (1917), *Plantain (Podorozhnik)* (1921), and *Anno Domini MCMXXI* (1922). There is also a long poem written in 1914 and published separately in 1921, *At the Very Edge of the Sea*.

A convenient, readily accessible and representative collection of these works is the Chekhov Press edition (New York, 1952), *Selected Poems*. Although this edition is inferior in many respects to later Soviet and Western collections, it has the advantage of reproducing almost entirely the first editions of the individual works.

Akhmatova's poetry is of an unusually personal nature in that it contains a great many references and reminiscences of an autobiographical character. The typically laconic style does not permit elaboration of such references, and the result is a certain obscurity in a poetry which is generally praised for its simplicity and clarity. The first chapter, therefore, includes a biographical sketch of the poet, at least for the years which are under special consideration. Certain details, otherwise insignificant, appear here because of direct references to them in the poems. While a purely autobiographical reading is by no means suggested, this information may provide a background for interpreting some of Akhmatova's poems. The second half of the chapter, dealing with the period 1922 to the present, is a literary biography: a survey of Akhmatova's literary production, including the poet's long and gallant struggle against literary regimentation. There follows an analysis of Akhmatova's early poetry, with especial attention to themes and lexicon, and a brief commentary on the relationship between the early works and the major works of the later period.

Acknowledgments

I should like to acknowledge my very great debt to Professor Leon Stilman for his careful reading of the dissertation manuscript on which this book is based, and for saving me from mistakes and misinterpretations which I am afraid were rather numerous. Any errors in the present version are of course my own. I should like to thank also Professors Richard Gregg and Rufus Mathewson for their very valuable help and encouragement. I am indebted also to Mrs. Irene Kirk and Miss Amanda Haight for helping me communicate with Akhmatova. For her kindness and generosity during the difficult stages of this writing, my very especial thanks go to Dr. Faith Sweet (Mrs. Henry Stearns).

Providence, R.I.

Contents

Chronology

1889 June 11. Anna Andreevna Gorenko born in Bolshoy Fontan, near Odessa. Family moved to Pavlovsk; finally settles in Tsarskoe Selo.

1889– Grows up in Tsarskoe Selo, spends summers with family on Black
1906 Sea. Attends girl's Gymnasium at Tsarskoe Selo. Comes under influence of Innokenty Annensky; forms a close relationship with Nikolay Gumilyov.

1906– Studies for a year in Kiev; by 1907 returns for advanced literary
1907 study in Petersburg.

1907 First publication of Akhmatova's poetry in Gumilyov's journal *Sirius,* in Paris.

1910 Spends spring in Paris.

1911 Marries Gumilyov, returns to Paris. Moves in artistic and literary circles.

1912 Travels in northern Italy. Publication of first collection of poems, *Evening.* Season spent in Petersburg literary society, springs abroad, and summers at Slepnyovo, Gumilyov's country estate. Son, Lev, born.

1913 Last year of peace; in Akhmatova's poetry, final year of the old way of life.

1914 Publication of second volume of poems, *The Rosary.* Long poem, *At the Very Edge of the Sea,* written. Gumilyov enlists in calvary with declaration of war; later decorated for bravery.

1917 Publication of *The White Flock,* third volume of poems, mostly written during summers at Slepnyovo. Gumilyov transferred to administrative post in London, then in Paris; he returns immediately on learning of Communist takeover.

1918 Akhmatova and Gumilyov divorced. Akhmatova retires from literary society. Works in Agronomy Institute, later in a series of publishing houses.

1921 Publication of poetry collection, *Plantain,* and poem, *At the Very Edge of the Sea.* Akhmatova comes out of seclusion to read her latest volume, *Anno Domini MCMXXI.* In August, appears at funeral of Alexander Blok. In that same month, Gumilyov, who had been arrested for counterrevolutionary activity, is executed. Akhmatova becomes part of the "inner emigration."

1922 *Anno Domini MCMXXI* published.

1923– Akhmatova publishes no new work during this period, but is
1929   subject of critical studies and disputes.

1929– Akhmatova's poetry not published, but some of her scholarly
1939   work appears. In consequence of repression, Akhmatova's twenty-
        year-old son Lev arrested in 1934, but soon released. In 1937, Lev
        jailed again, but permitted to join military service after war begins.

1940   Akhmatova again published; latest volume, *From Six Books,*
        contains completely new cycle of poems. Edition, however, recalled
        after six months.

1941   Siege of Leningrad. Akhmatova in Leningrad through bombard-
        ment; evacuated to Moscow, then Tashkent. Remains in Tashkent
        until 1944.

1942   Akhmatova's war poem "Courage" printed in *Pravda* and widely
        circulated. Akhmatova fully "rehabilitated."

1942– Publication of poems in various journals; by 1945, journals *Zvezda*
1945   and *Leningrad* proclaim Akhmatova first among Leningrad poets.
        Edition of complete works being prepared.

1946   Central Committee of CPSU reimposes regimentation of literature
        by attacking journals *Zvezda* and *Leningrad*; Comrade Zhdanov
        launches vicious attack on Akhmatova and Zoshchenko. Articles
        attacking Akhmatova follow; she is expelled from Writer's Union,
        and can no longer be published.

1949   As culmination of new terroristic campaign against Akhmatova,
        her son is again imprisoned, sentenced to fifteen years of exile and
        hard labor. He is finally released only in 1956.

1950   Publication of cycle, *In Praise of Peace,* a series of poems similar
        to "Soviet" poetry, presumably written to help Lev's position. Other
        original works not published until "the Thaw."

1951– Publication of number of translations from various languages,
1956   including entire volume of Korean classical poetry.

1956– Original poetry again published in newspapers and journals. In
1958   1958, *Poems,* first new volume of selected works since 1922 is pub-
        lished (discounting 1940 edition, which was recalled). Rehabilitation
        gradually made complete.

1960   Publication of still another collection, *Poems,* including many new
        works.

1964   Travels to Catania, Italy; receives Taormina Poetry Prize. Awarded
        an honorary degree at Oxford. Visits Paris.

1965   Publication of major collection under title, *The Course of Time*
        (*Beg vremeni*), including selections from early volumes as well as
        new works.

1966   Appearance of first book-length study of Akhmatova in the Soviet
        Union since 1920's. March 5: Dies. Official honors. Burial at Koma-
        rovo, village near Leningrad, where Akhmatova spent her last years.

CHAPTER 1

Literary Biography

ANNA Akhmatova was born Anna Andreevna Gorenko near Odessa (Bolshoy Fontan) on June 11, 1889. She was to choose as a pseudonym her grandmother's name, which is of Tatar origin. She kept her Christian name.

> *I was at that time visiting the earth.*
> *They gave me at my christening the name Anna,*
> *The sweetest one for human lips and hearing. . . . (217)[1]*

At the time of Akhmatova's birth, her father had retired as a maritime engineer. The family moved from the shore of the Black Sea to Pavlovsk, an Imperial summer residence near Petersburg. Shortly thereafter, Akhmatova's father settled his family in Tsarskoe Selo—"my toy town," as Akhmatova was later to call it (6).

This old town, with its handsome houses neatly laid out on shady streets near the gardens of the magnificent baroque Summer Palace, is remembered with fondness and nostalgia both in her poetry and in an autobiographical note: "My first memories are of Tsarskoe Selo: the green, damp magnificence of the parks, the commons where my nurse used to take me, the hippodrome where small, motley horses galloped, the old station. . . ."[2]

Tsarskoe Selo, the Versailles of Catherine the Great, stands as a monument to classical measure in Russian art. It was there, at the famous Lycée in a wing attached to the palace, that Akhmatova's beloved Pushkin composed his remarkable youthful works. The palace and gardens hold at every step memories of the great poet.

> *The swarthy youth wandered in these allees*
> *Near the deserted lake banks*
> *And for a century we have cherished*
> *The barely audible rustle of his steps.*

Pine needles dense and prickly
Cover the low stumps . . .
Here lay his three-cornered hat
And a ruffled volume of Parny. (225)

Here in Tsarskoe Selo, at the age of eleven, the young Anna wrote her first poem.

Akhmatova recalls her childhood as a carefree, happy time despite the family's financial worries and the growing strain between the parents because of them. Her recollections are bright against the predominantly somber background of her poetry. She describes herself as a rather solitary child; her fondest memories of childhood are those connected with summers spent near Sevastopol on the Black Sea. She was a good swimmer, and proud of her ability. If solitary, she does not seem to have been a lonely child, and the years passed untroubled. She "grew up in the patterned quiet, In the young century's cool nursery . . ."(9).

The school years were spent mostly in Tsarskoe Selo. Akhmatova was at first a poor student, and although she improved greatly later, she was never a willing one. She left the girls' Gymnasium in Tsarskoe Selo at sixteen to complete her final year at a Gymnasium in Kiev. She was graduated in 1906, and entered the University of Kiev's Law School. Although Latin, a required subject, interested her, she was bored with law. She transferred to Petersburg for advanced studies in literature.

I *Akhmatova and Gumilyov*

The year of Akhmatova's graduation from the Gymnasium saw the first publication of her poetry. It appeared in *Sirius,* a short-lived[3] literary journal published in Paris by her future husband, Nikolay Gumilyov.[4] Akhmatova and Gumilyov had become acquainted while both were students at the Gymnasiums in Tsarskoe Selo. It was the beginning of a tragic love which became the most important single theme in Akhmatova's poetry up to 1922.

After school, they would walk along the wooded paths of Tsarskoe Selo. Gumilyov recalls:

The young couple would walk down the allee,
so strangely tender,
Schoolboy and schoolgirl, like Daphnis and Chloe.

Akhmatova writes of those early days at a time when her relationship to Gumilyov was already changing.

> *My books and pencil-case strapped together,*
> *I was walking home from school:*
> *These lindens surely haven't forgotten*
> *Our first meeting, my gay lad.*
> *Only, having become a haughty swan,*
> *The grey cygnet changed.*[5]

The young students discovered that they shared an enthusiasm
for poetry,[6] for Innokenty Annensky, in particular.

Annensky, a gifted poet, critic and Hellenist, lived in Tsarskoe
Selo where he was director of the boys' Gymnasium from 1896
to 1905.[7] He remained in Tsarskoe Selo until his death in 1909.
The last year of his life he gave lectures on literature in Petersburg,
which Akhmatova attended. Annensky had a particular interest
in feminine lyricists;[8] Akhmatova soon came under his tutelage.

When Akhmatova was shown the proofs of Annensky's book,
The Cypress Coffer (Kiparisovy larets), she wrote that she was
"overcome, and read it having forgotten everything else on earth."[9]
Gumilyov, who could be haughty and arrogant with other poets,
describes himself as "timid" before the author of *The Cypress
Coffer*.[10]

Outside the world of poetry, Akhmatova and Gumilyov seemed,
from all accounts, to have had little in common. In physical appearance, they were an oddly matched couple,[11] and their personalities
seemed quite incompatible.

Although both were essentially solitary types from childhood,[12]
and were in some respects to remain so for the rest of their lives,
even solitude was for each radically different in mood and nature.
Akhmatova sought her solitude in the woman's world of hearth
and garden, in the quiet understanding of a small circle of close
friends, and in the peace of being surrounded with familiar things.
The imagery of home is important to Akhmatova's poetry; homelessness is the symbol for ultimate tragedy.

To Gumilyov, home is a prison, and personal attachments
are fetters. His first published poem stated a characteristic theme
of escape which was to flow through his later work and set a pattern
for his life.

Escape from the contemporary world into medieval history,

classical literature and mythology, and into the study of exotic lands was typical for Gumilyov's Symbolist predecessors. Often, there was real scholarship involved, as in Annensky's case, but sometimes it was merely the search for the exotic. Gumilyov, despite a certain pretention, was not a true scholar, nor was he satisfied just to read about far lands and customs. His early poetry reflects a desire, almost a compulsion, to escape home, family duty, Russia, and even Europe itself, for the freedom of distant lands. How much his desire was spontaneous and how much conditioned by his reading of contemporary French and Russian poets is difficult to say.[13]

Both poets disliked ordinary, that is, non-literary society, but where Akhmatova preferred to withdraw quietly into herself, Gumilyov often disguised his reticence with arrogance, and not infrequently, in a show of bravado, would precipitate some scandal and thus deliberately make himself the center of attention.

"Akhmatova was always withdrawn, an outsider everywhere. . . . She came alive only when the conversation concerned poetry."[14] Gumilyov, on the other hand, seemed to have vacillated between a cold aloofness and an apparently compulsive periodic *engagement*.[15] His contemporaries remember him as either morosely taciturn or amiably gregarious. Gumilyov had already established in Tsarskoe Selo a reputation as a fop and tireless Don Juan— traits which were to remain characteristic through most of his life.[16]

There seem to be as many explanations for Gumilyov's inconsistent behavior as there are critics who wrote about him. Otsup suggests the Byronic clubfoot as one possible reason;[17] Yuly Aykhenvald accepts Gumilyov as the *persona* of his poems, "the last of the conquistadors, a poet-warrior, a poet-cuirassier, with the soul of a Viking. . . ."[18] Georgy Ivanov knew Gumilyov for a "naturally timid, gentle, sickly and bookish man," whose conflict arose from an indomitable will "to be the first in any human endeavor."[19] Ivanov noted that Gumilyov was inordinately proud even as a youngster, driven by an ambition to lead and a desire for fame.[20]

Whatever lay at the basis of Gumilyov's character—psychological complex, a literary pose enacted in life, or the "will principle"—[21] it seemed from the outset that any lasting relationship with Akhmatova was improbable.[22] They had, essentially, only their poetry in common, and with Akhmatova's later successes, the poetry itself perhaps became a source of contention with him.

In 1906, Akhmatova left Tsarskoe Selo for Kiev to complete her last year of Gymnasium there. Gumilyov was finally graduated in 1907 and left immediately for Paris, where he studied at the Sorbonne. Here, he organized the ill-fated *Sirius*. In 1908, he made his first trip to Africa, to Egypt and the Sudan. Returning to Paris, he published his second collection of verse *Romanticheskie tsvety* (*Romantic Flowers*). It was dedicated to Akhmatova.

Gumilyov spent the winter months 1909-10 again in Africa, this time in Abyssinia. The following spring, he returned to Russia, and that spring, he and Akhmatova were married. Gumilyov wrote: "From a nest of vipers,/From the city of Kiev,/I took not a wife, but a witch. . . ."[23]

After a wedding trip to Paris, Gumilyov and Akhmatova returned to spend the summer—and the three succeeding ones—at Slepnyovo, a small estate belonging to Gumilyov's mother. The estate was deep in the Russian countryside, in the province of Tver. The household was a matriarchal one, presided over by Gumilyov's archconservative mother, and included as permanent guests a number of aged aunts and cousins.

Akhmatova recalled the landscape in 1961: "It is not a picturesque place: fields plowed in even squares on the hilly ground, mills, quagmires, drained swamps, 'farmgates,' and grain, grain. . . ."[24]

In some rather gossipy reminiscences, a former neighbor to Slepnyovo describes the young couple's early married life in the country.

I remember now my first impression on meeting Gumilyov and Akhmatova at their Slepnoyovo estate. Gumilyov came from the garden onto the veranda where we were drinking tea; on his head was a lemon-yellow fez, and on his feet lilac socks and sandals, and with all that, a Russian peasant's shirt. Later, I came to realize that Gumilyov in general loved the grotesque in life— and in dress. He had an unusual face—intelligent, penetrating eyes, slightly crossed. His manners were exaggeratedly ceremonious; his eyes and mouth were rather derisive; one could sense that he wanted to scandalize and mock his good aunts, all this tea-drinking with jam, and the conversations about the weather, harvest, and so on.

Akhmatova had the stern face of a novice in an Old Believer's convent. Her features were too sharp to call the face beautiful. Her grey eyes were without a smile. She must have been about twenty-one or twenty-two. She sat silent at the table, and one could sense immediately that she was an outsider in her husband's family. In that matriarchal household, both Nikolay Stepanovich and his wife were fish out of water. His mother was aggrieved that her son had not wanted to serve in the guards or the dip-lomatic corps, but, had become a poet—who vanishes off to Africa—and besides that, brings home some queer sort of wife who also writes poetry, never says anything, dresses now in dark homespun, now in extravagant Paris get-ups (in those days they wore hobbleskirts). Of course, the success of [Akhmatova's] *Rosary* created an impression on the family, but the estrangement remained the same.[25]

In this environment, Akhmatova wrote a good part of her second[26] volume *Rosary* (1914) and almost the whole of the *White Flock* (1917). The former collection contains this poem, which gives ex-pression to Akhmatova's dominant mood at Slepnyovo:

> *You know, I languish, imprisoned,*
> *Praying the Lord for death.*
> *But painfully present is the memory*
> *Of the meager land of Tver'.*
>
> *The crane at the dilapidated well,*
> *Above it, like foam, the clouds,*
> *In the fields, the creaking little gates,*
> *And the smell of grain, and the longing.*
>
> *And those indistinct, open spaces,*
> *Where even the voice of the wind is weak,*
> *And the condemning glances*
> *Of calm, sunburned peasant women.* (194)

The mood reflected in this poem, if apparently the dominant one during the long Slepnyovo summers, was not entirely unrelieved: as long as Gumilyov was at Slepnyovo, Akhmatova's life could be at times trying, but never boring. Mme Nevedomskaya, on whose neighboring estate the young couple were frequent guests, recalls the summer of 1912. The Nevedomskys kept a stable, and Gumilyov was particularly fond of riding—although "Nikolay Stepanovich, practically speaking, did not know how to ride at all; he had a complete lack of fear. He would mount any horse, stand on the saddle and go through the most skull-splitting antics."

The young Gumilyovs introduced an element of the bizarre and fantastic into the long, dull summer days of their neighbors. Gumilyov wrote weird plays in verse, and directed the local gentry in their production. He invented madcap pranks, scandalizing the older generation. Once, he organized a travelling circus, and devised fantastic costumes for the participants. They rode over to the next estate and put on an impromptu show for the peasants, who cheerfully passed the hat for their efforts. In the circus, "Anna was billed as the snake-woman. She was extraordinarily supple, and easily placed her leg behind her neck and touched the nape with her heel—preserving throughout the severe mien of a religious novice."

This picture, so at odds with the public image of the tragic poet, indicates that Akhmatova did not always take herself entirely seriously. Flashes of subtle humor and quiet whimsy are not infrequent in her verse, and she was not above parodying the style she used in the most somber of her poems.[27]

In the winter, Gumilyov and Akhmatova lived in Tsarskoe Selo, in the house of Gumilyov's mother. It was a large, handsome old house, somewhat musty inside, with an old garden and orangery. Within the household, life must have been not much different from that at Slepnyovo. There were, however, literary evenings in Tsarskoe Selo and Petersburg, and here, Akhmatova was in her element. Frequently, the young couple held literary receptions, drawing on the fascinating world of the St. Petersburg poets. "The poets would gather: elegant Blok, Mikhail Kuzmin with his downcast eyes, Klyuev, shaven bald and noticeably shy of society; Count Komarovsky, shortly before dismissed from a clinic for the mentally ill. . . ."[28] Akhmatova, usually so reticent, entered willingly into the "acid humor of the literary joke" (161).

Akhmatova and Gumilyov also attended the literary salons and receptions of St. Petersburg, and the especially fashionable "evenings" of Sergey Gorodetsky.

The meeting place of poets, painters, Bohemians, and the late-hours-society of the city was the *Brodyachaya sobaka* (The Roving Dog). This fabulous *cave* was a low, dark basement, its windows sealed against the world outside, and its walls painted with fantastic birds and flowers. Here, poets scribbled verse and read it aloud; literary discussions lasted far into the night.

Gumilyov was respected here, but held himself apart. Akhmatova more and more often began to appear alone. Georgy Ivanov recalls

her sitting withdrawn and aloof from the admiring ladies in big
flowered hats who surrounded her. Akhmatova would sit until
the early hours of the morning, and here she wrote one of her
most famous poems, "Cabaret artistique," on New Year's Eve,
1913: "We're all revellers here, and harlots,/How joyless we are
together!/Flowers and birds on the walls/Long for the clouds . . ."
(177).

Following the winter seasons in Petersburg, Akhmatova and
Gumilyov again went abroad in the spring of 1911 and 1912.
Akhmatova was not the enthusiastic traveller that Gumilyov was,
but she recalls the months spent in Paris with pleasure. She witnessed
the first triumphs of Diaghilev's ballet,[29] and spent many hours in
conversation with Modigliani.

In 1912, Gumilyov and Akhmatova toured Northern Italy
(Genoa, Pisa, Florence, Bologna, Padua, and Venice). Akhmatova
wrote in 1960: "My impression of Italian painting and architecture
was immense; it is like a dream which you remember all your life."[30]
Akhmatova had a deep and abiding interest in painting; in 1937,
she translated and annotated the letters of Rubens.[31]

After the Italian tour, Gumilyov left Akhmatova once again for
Africa; this time going to Abyssinia. Their marriage by this time
was already quite strained.[32]

In the same year of 1912, Akhmatova's first collection of verse
appeared, It was *Vecher (Evening)*, for which Mikhail Kuzmin
wrote an introduction; Sergey Gorodetsky designed the cover.
Only three hundred copies were printed; the book could not have
been a popular success, but the critics reacted most favorably.[33]

Akhmatova, as the wife of Gumilyov, was already well-known in
the poetic circles of St. Petersburg. Her formal introduction as a
poet had taken place the year before, in "The Tower." This was the
name which, for more than one good reason, was given to the apartment of Vyacheslav Ivanov—poet, scholar, mentor and "high
priest" of the Russian Symbolist movement.

Ivanov received the members of the literary world who were interesting
and akin to him. With his wife . . . he began to hold receptions every
Wednesday in his modest apartment on the sixth floor of a house on Taurida
Park. The building was a high corner house, and the windows opened
onto the two streets below, like a kind of beacon. Hence, the quickly-
established famous name, "The Tower." Every Wednesday . . . the Russian

Symbolists came, bringing their new achievements for judgment and praise. . . . They were not just in "The Tower"; they had reached the heights.[34]

Akhmatova began to frequent the Tower in 1911. The "master" noticed her work, and once, at a chance meeting, even expressed his approval of a short lyric poem which was to become one of her most famous:

> *How helplessly my heart grew cold,*
> *But my steps were light.*
> *I drew onto my right hand*
> *My left-hand glove.*
>
> *There seemed so many steps,*
> *Though I knew there were but three!*
> *From the maples, an autumn rustling*
> *Said, "Die with me!*
>
> *I've been deceived by my despairing,*
> *Treacherous, evil fate."*
> *I answered, "Dear one!*
> *So have I. I'll die with you . . . ."*
>
> *This is the song of the last meeting.*
> *I looked at the darkened house.*
> *Only in the bedroom candles burned*
> *With an indifferent yellow light.*[35]

The success, in the following year, of Akhmatova's *Evening* supported Ivanov's intuition. Her second little volume, *Rosary,* was published in 1914 and delighted the public as well as the critics. Despite publishing difficulties during the war and revolution, *Rosary* went into nine editions.[36] By 1914, there were already signs of an "Akhmatova school" among young Russian poets.[37] *Rosary* had captured the hearts of a whole generation.

Marina Tsvetaeva, the other major woman-poet of the period, said that she could not have written her poems about Moscow if Akhmatova had not first written of Petersburg. "I read all my work of 1915. . . . I sense clearly that I am reading the work of a Muscovite (and I wish to) raise it to the level of an Akhmatova. Akhmatova! The word is said. With all my being, I feel an intense and inevitable

comparison with Akhmatova in every single line of mine . . . ."
Tsvetaeva cites this poem from 1916: "In my singing city, the
cupolas flame,/And a wandering blind man praises the Glorious
Saviour,/ And I give to you my bell-towered city / Akhmatova!—and
my own heart in the bargain. . . ."[38]

As Akhmatova's popularity and influence increased, her relationship with Gumilyov became more and more strained. From all
accounts,[39] it appears that Gumilyov resented his wife's almost
immediate success. It is significant that in all Gumilyov's twenty-
four "Letters about Russian Poetry" and seven articles on poetry
which Gumilyov contributed to the journal *Apollon,*[40] he discusses
Akhmatova's work in only one. He reviews *Chyotki* briefly in Letter
XXII; it is perceptive, but notably condescending in tone.

Insofar as Akhmatova's own poetry can be taken as evidence,
Gumilyov's attitude toward her writing seems clear enough: "You
don't want children from me/And you don't like my poems" (76).
"He was talking about the summer and/About how absurd it is for
a woman to be a poet" (188).[41]

Gumilyov's poems also reflect the growing estrangement in his
marriage, if much less frequently than Akhmatova's. In "By the
Hearth," written some time during the first two years of their
marriage, Gumilyov repeats his theme of home as prison.
He recalls the freedom of his travels and says, "I have learned,
I have learned, what fear is./ Being buried here within four walls . . .
/And, malicious triumph concealed in her eyes,/The woman in
the corner was listening to him."[42]

In the spring of 1913, Gumilyov again went to Africa, where
he spent six months as head of an ethnographic expedition to Abyssinia and Somaliland.[43] On his return to Petersburg, he and Akhmatova were united only for a short time: within a month after the
declaration of war, Gumilyov enlisted. Typically, he chose the most
dangerous service, the cavalry—he was the only prominent literary
figure to join the cavalry.

Gumilyov saw action almost immediately, was twice commended
for bravery, was awarded the cross of St. George, and was granted
a battlefield commission.[44]

Akhmatova and her son Lev, who had been born in 1912, stayed
with Gumilyov's family at the old house in Tsarskoe Selo and in
the summertime at Slepnyovo.

One afternoon in the winter of 1916, Georgy Ivanov called on

Akhmatova in Tsarskoe Selo. Gumilyov was at the Front. They talked of the heavy losses that winter. Ivanov asked Akhmatova to recite a poem. "My poems," she answered, "are boring nowadays . . .

> *Sleep, my quiet one, sleep, my son,*
> *I am a bad mother.*
> *News rarely reaches*
> *Our front porch.*
> *They gave your father*
> *A little white cross.*
> *There has been grief, there will be grief,*
> *To grief there is no end.*
> *May Saint George protect*
> *Your father. . . ."*[45]

In 1917, Gumilyov was transferred in an administrative capacity to London, and later to Paris. In Paris, he learned of the outbreak of the Revolution, and returned directly to Russia through Murmansk.

Akhmatova was no longer living with her husband's family at Tsarskoe Selo when Gumilyov returned. The marriage, after faltering for almost six years, could not survive the last long separation. In 1918, they were divorced.

A year later, Gumilyov married Anna Nikolaevna Engelhardt, and Akhmatova was married briefly to Vladimir Kazimirovich Shileyko (1891–1930), a brilliant Assyriologist, who was also a poet.[46]

II *The War Years*

By the time *Podorozhnik (Plantain)* was published in 1921,[47] Akhmatova was alone, and the world she had known had been shattered by the Revolution. In this collection with the humblest of titles, impressions of those violent days are intermixed with her deep personal loss.

After the October Revolution, Akhmatova retired almost completely from literary society. She worked for a time in the library of the Agronomy Institute, and later in a number of publishing houses.

Fantastic rumors about Akhmatova's fate circulated in émigré literary groups, but there is little accurate information concerning her during the years immediately following the Revolution. One anecdote among the reminiscences of Vladislav Khodasevich must have been typical of Akhmatova's life in those hard years. Rations were distributed weekly to Petersburg writers at the House of Scholars. The food packets were of varying quantity and quality, and sometimes there were none at all. Once, after several weeks without rations, the writers suddenly received a packet: eighteen pounds of herring. Khodasevich carried his herring to the market place to sell or barter for necessities. Opening his bag to display his merchandise, he noticed at some distance a tall figure standing silently beside a bag like his own. It was Akhmatova, selling herring in the noisy market place on the Obvodny Canal. . . .[48]

Akhmatova had come out of seclusion once during these difficult years. In the spring of 1921, it was announced that she was to read a major new work at the *Dom literatorov* (House of Writers). It was *Anno Domini MCMXXI*. The public hall of the *Dom literatorov* could not accommodate a tenth of the people who came; the reading had to be repeated in a huge auditorium at the University. Georgy Ivanov felt that the new book was not well-received, that Akhmatova's characteristically severe poetry had become too severe for an audience which had come to hear of new "left-hand gloves being drawn onto the right." Contemporary reviewers, however, held a quite different opinion; the new work was an extraordinary success.[49]

Akhmatova again went into seclusion. Some six months later, in August 1921, she appeared alone, ill, and grief-stricken, at the funeral of Alexander Blok.

Blok, the last and greatest of the Symbolists, had once been fairly close to both Akhmatova and Gumilyov, and had attended at least one of the meetings of the "Poets' Workshop." Although Blok cooled toward Gumilyov and his group after the publication of their manifestoes, he remained well-disposed toward Akhmatova until his death.[50] While there appears to be no truth in the persistent rumor that there was something more than just friendship in Akhmatova's relationship with Blok,[51] she was nevertheless deeply affected by his tragic death. She wrote this moving dirge, with its strong overtones of the Russian folk tradition:

> *And today is the nameday of Our Lady of Smolensk,*
> *Blue incense spreads over the grass,*
> *And the singing of the requiem streams,*

> *Not sad now, but serene.*
> *And the rosy-cheeked widows bring*
> *Their little boys and girls to the cemetery*
> *To look at the graves of their fathers,*
> *And the cemetery is a nightingale grove,*
> *Stilled by the shining of the sun.*
> *We brought to the Intercessor of Smolensk,*
> *We brought to the Most Holy Virgin,*
> *Holding in a silver casket*
> *Our sun, extinguished in torment—*
> *Alexander, the pure swan.* (52)

The shock of Blok's death was followed almost immediately by an even greater one. Barely two weeks after Blok's funeral, Gumilyov was executed as a counterrevolutionary.

When Gumilyov returned to Russia after the Revolution, he had become a member of the editorial board of the World Literature publishing house founded by Gorky. After 1919, he taught in several literary studios, reformed the "Poets' Workshop" and became its president. While he worked tirelessly and with great pleasure teaching the Baltic Fleet sailors and the struggling poets of the Proletkult (Proletarian Cultural and Educational Organizations, founded in September, 1917), Gumilyov did not hesitate to criticize the regime, and expounded his monarchist views openly.

In June of 1921, Gumilyov made a short trip to Sevastopol in the Crimea. It seems quite possible, and even likely, that he was involved in a counterrevolutionary movement later known as the "Tagantsev affair," establishing contacts with convalescing officers and distributing anti-Soviet leaflets in Crimean ports. On August 3, 1921, Gumilyov was arrested and charged with participation in the conspiracy. Attempts by major literary figures to have Gumilyov released ended in failure.[52] He was shot on August 24, 1921.

Akhmatova once more went into seclusion, and was to publish no original poetry for almost two decades. In 1922, when many writers and intellectuals were leaving Russia, Georgy Ivanov came to say goodbye to Akhmatova:

> —*You are leaving? Say hello to Paris for me.*
> *And you, Anna Andreevna, aren't you getting*
> *ready to go?*
> —*No, I shall not leave Russia.*
> —*But really, it's becoming more and more*
> *difficult to live.*

—Yes, more difficult.
—It might become completely unbearable.
—What is to be done?
—You aren't leaving?
—I shall not leave.[53]

In a poetic expression of her determination, Akhmatova wrote: ". . . Forever pitiable to me is the exile,/As a prisoner is, or a sick man./Dark is your path, wanderer,/Foreign bread smells of wormwood . . ." (41).

III *After War and Revolution*

Akhmatova, like many other writers, chose to join the "inner emigration." By 1922, she retired entirely from life, although she continued to write. Also like many other authors, she found refuge in scholarship. She writes in her autobiographical note: "From about the mid-twenties, I began earnestly and with great interest to study the architecture of old Petersburg and the life and works of Pushkin. The results of my Pushkin studies were three works— about the 'Golden Cockerel,' about Benjamin Constant's *Adolphe,* and about "'The Stone Guest.'"

Apparently, toward the end of the 1920's, Akhmatova received an offer to publish her collected works. The "Izdatelstvo Pisateley v Leningrade" (Writers' Publishing House in Leningrad) received permission from the censor to publish in two volumes the collected works of Akhmatova—under the editorship of the third-rate, but at that time politically all-powerful poet, Demyan Bedny. This arrangement would be something like Edgar Guest's writing a preface to the collected verse of Marianne Moore. "Akhmatova categorically refused this honor, preferring to remain unpublished."[54]

Although Akhmatova herself went into seclusion after the tragic events of 1921, and after 1922 was no longer published, her name did not disappear from the literary scene. On the contrary, up to 1929—the time of the complete regimentation of literature— her works were even more prominent in the critical world than ever before. Akhmatova's delicate lyrics became favorite material for scholars and critics, especially of the so-called Formalist school, which concerned itself with problems of metrics, semantics, and linguistics.[55]

Akhmatova's attitude toward the complex systems built upon the fragile material of her verse emerges quite clearly in her poetry; her reaction to fame was not a modest deprecation but downright contempt. "And in the morning, fame will drag along, to shake a child's rattle in my ear ..." (49); "The praise of this earth is like smoke; I didn't ask for it ..." (77); "so you want fame? ... It is a trap wherein there is neither happiness nor light ..." (156). Akhmatova called her fame "my unglorious glory." She chose a literary evening devoted to her poetry as a setting for a poem which begins: "The tongue-tied man who was celebrating me/Was still stamping around on the edge of the stage./We were all, of course, glad to leave/The blue-grey smoke and the dreary lights ..." (179).

Despite the near-adulation of Akhmatova during the first years of her silence, a quite different brand of criticism was beginning to develop: official, or Party-line, criticism. It was this hack criticism which was to play a decisive and often central role in Akhmatova's life.

In the early 1920's, the battle between Formalist and Party critics often centered upon the verse of Akhmatova. As early as 1920, V. Chudovsky noted that "all Russia is now split between Akhmatova supporters and Mayakovsky supporters. Between these groups is a gulf of a millenium. And they hate each other."[56] Oksyonov seconded this view: "These two names—Akhmatova and Mayakovsky—are in reality symbols of the split in modern poetry (and not only in poetry). These names define two different creative paths, different world-views and different faiths. ..."[57]

The Party critics themselves, who could agree on Mayakovsky as the voice of the Revolution, were by no means unanimous in their evaluation of Akhmatova. They varied from proclaiming her a "voice of the people" to condemning her categorically as a bourgeois relic. A middle group, while criticizing Akhmatova's lack of "social purpose," could not help admiring her work. Lvov-Rogachevsky, writing as late as 1925, is typical of this middle group.[58] An article in *Pravda* which stated that "after the death of Blok, the first place among Russian poets belongs undisputedly to Anna Akhmatova"[59] was scathingly attacked by G. Lelevich, critic and theoretician of the "On Guard" movement in the Association of Proletarian Writers.[60] While Lelevich ridiculed the "bourgeois" nature of Akhmatova's poetry, he did note her technical ability. Georgy Gorbachyov, a fellow On-Guardist of Lelevich, who also derided "bourgeois" poetry, nevertheless recognized

Akhmatova as the most talented of her school, and agreed entirely
with Eykhenbaum's highly favorable opinion.[61]

An extreme wing objected strongly to this compromise view of
the middle group. The first of this extreme wing to comment on
Akhmatova, V. Arvatov, wrote on a pitifully low critical level;[62]
nevertheless, his views were parroted by later critics, notably Viktor
Pertsov.[63] Even Zhdanov, in later years, seems to have been hard
put to add anything to Arvatov's article, other than violence and
vulgarity.

Apart from the professional critics, Akhmatova was much discussed during this period of her silence by writers, poets, and
litterateurs as well. Eykhenvald composed a verbal portrait of the
poetess as she emerges in her work,[64] and poems were dedicated
to her by Tinyakov, Lozinsky, Gollerbakh, and Tsvetaeva, as
Blok, Komarovsky, Kuzmin, Gumilyov, and Mandelstam had
done earlier.[65]

Typical of the awareness of Akhmatova in the public mind during
this period was a dispute which appeared on the pages of *Molodaya
Gvardiya (The Young Guard)*. The polemics involved the famous
Tovarishch Kollontay and the early Party critic, Arvatov. Their
articles represented the first shift away from the earlier scholarly
and critical studies to a strictly socio-political approach in which
Akhmatova's poetry served merely as a springboard for the critic's
views.[66]

Although Akhmatova held aloof from all the literary battles
of the 1920's, and although the view represented by Arvatov
became the only possible one, she was far from forgotten by her
public. During the 1930's, there was no possibility of the preceding
decade's angry critical battles, but the dissatisfaction with literary
production had become general. More importantly, with the Second
World War imminent, Party leaders felt that controls on literature
should be relaxed.

Almost immediately, Akhmatova's poetry reappeared. In 1940
an edition of her earlier works, including a completely new cycle,
was published.[67]

The attempt at rehabilitation, however, was premature; the
new collection appeared in bookstores and libraries for a bare
six months, when it was covertly recalled.[68]

IV *The Second World War and After*

Akhmatova was living in Leningrad when the war began for Russia in 1941. She remained there through the terrible bombardment, before the siege. In late September, she was evacuated to Moscow and then to Tashkent. During the war years, she wrote some magnificent poems about Russia and particularly about Leningrad. Emigrés from the Soviet Union recall that during that terrible winter of famine, cold, and shelling, Akhmatova's war poetry was copied and circulated in manuscript; it was recited in the bomb shelters and it gave heart to many inhabitants of the beleaguered city.

Aleksey Surkov, in an article included in the 1961 edition of Akhmatova's selected works, testifies to the place Akhmatova's war poems held in the early years of the war:

... And so, in February of 1942, when the Fascist hordes were blockading Leningrad and when they had just barely been thrown back from the walls of Moscow and were still fighting desperately in the South and Southeast, Akhmatova's poem "Courage" appeared in the pages of *Pravda,* alongside military communiqués and correspondence from the Front. ...

I remember, in the bitter winter days of 1942, when I was speaking on Soviet war poetry in the Hall of Columns of the *Dom Soyuzov,* I read this poem to the accompaniment of air-raid sirens. The stern audience, two-thirds military men, greeted it with an applause which did not abate for a long time.[69]

By 1945, the journals *Zvezda (Star)* and *Leningrad,* which had been printing Akhmatova's poetry, proclaimed her the best among the group called the "Leningrad Poets."

Shortly after Akhmatova's arrival in the capital September 1941, she was evacuated on official orders to Tashkent. In her autobiographical sketch, she writes that there she grasped hungrily for news of Leningrad, of the Front.

Like other poets, I frequently read in hospitals to the wounded soldiers. In Tashkent I first learned what the shade of trees and the sound of water mean. And I also learned what man's kindness is: in Tashkent, I was often and seriously ill.

In May of 1944, Akhmatova flew back to Moscow, which was already filled with the hope and expectation of victory. In June, she returned to Leningrad.

In 1945, in an interview with *Literaturnaya gazeta, (Literary Gazette)*, Akhmatova told the reporter that a complete edition of her works, including a yet unpublished volume, were in preparation for publication.

It seemed for a time that Akhmatova was firmly reinstated as a writer acceptable to the régime. The war was now over, and the relaxation of controls during the war had stimulated demands for still further literary freedom for Soviet writers.

The Soviet Union, after the devastation of the war, was in a desperate position. In a situation recalling the institution of the First Five-Year Plan in 1929, the Party leadership decided to channel all phases of Soviet life into the support of the Fourth Five-Year Plan, to begin in March, 1946. It was inevitable that the plan should be accompanied by "fresh ideological developments." The relative literary freedom of the war years had to be drastically curtailed— or, in the terms of the Soviet planners—"the plan must assume the further flowering of Soviet art and culture." Implementation of the plan for literature began with an incredibly vicious attack on Akhmatova and on Mikhail Zoshchenko, the famous writer and satirist, and on the journals which published their works. Together with the "Decision of the Central Committee Concerning the Journals *Zvezda* and *Leningrad* of August 14, 1946" was published the "Report of Comrade Zhdanov Concerning the Journals *Zvezda* and *Leningrad*."[70]

Although these two infamous documents are of surpassing importance to Akhmatova's life and career, there is little point in a close investigation of them here. Their contents are well-known, and even now, with something of a historical perspective, it is extremely distasteful to dwell on these violent, virulent diatribes.[71]

Perhaps because Zhdanov's *Report* had reached the extreme in injustice, vituperation, and Party cant, the spate of articles which dutifully followed read like parodies, and in some instances, one is tempted to believe that satire was intended. Viktor Pertsov, for example, who was both earlier and later favorable to Akhmatova,[72] turned on her in an article on Tvardovsky's wartime poem, "The House by the Side of the Road," ("Dom u dorogi"). He maintains that both poets are "against the People" *(antinarodnye)* because "they see war primarily as pain and suffering," and not as Comrade Stalin saw it, as a "school to test the fibre of the Russian people."[73]

Similarly absurd was the article by the new editor of *Zvezda,*

M.A. Egolin. Egolin selected Zhdanov's worst example of cant as a starting point: "... works (of Akhmatova) which are poisoned with the poison of zoological enmity to the Soviet order." This unusual enmity purportedly results from the fact that the "sympathies and ties of Akhmatova are on the side of the past." As an example of this deplorable state of affairs, Egolin cites—incredibly— Akhmatova's *Moy gorodok igrushechny sozhgli* ("They've burned my little toy town"), a touching poem written on the senseless destruction by the Germans of Tsarskoe Selo.[74]

Another article gives the following poem as an example of Akhmatova's *bezideynaya antinarodnost,* an untranslatable monument of Party jargon, which means literally "idea-less anti-Peopleness:"[75]

> There are trenches dug in the garden,
> And the lights are out.
> Petersburg orphans,
> Children mine.
>
> It's hard to breathe underground,
> Pain drills into the temples,
> Through the bombing is heard
> A child's thin voice. . . .

Akhmatova was expelled from the Union of Soviet Writers and was deprived of the right to publish. Once again she went into seclusion and lived in great hardship. According to the journal *Novy mir (New World),* the secret police persecuted Akhmatova throughout the late 1940's. As it often happened, prominent figures were made to suffer through persecution of those close to them. Her son, Lev Gumilyov, was imprisoned in 1949 and was sentenced to fifteen years of exile and hard labor.[76] *Novy mir* did not cite the charges brought against him; "presumably they were part of a terroristic campaign against Akhmatova."[77] Lev Gumilyov had been first arrested at the age of twenty in 1934 after the death of Kirov, but was soon released. In 1937 he was arrested again, and during the war was permitted to join the military service; he returned home in 1945. In the autumn of 1949, the Orientalist and scholar was rearrested and finally released only in May 1956.[78] His freedom was probably effected through a letter dated March 2, 1956, written by the Soviet author A.A. Fadeev, asking for a speedy

review of Lev Gumilyov's case.[79] In his appeal for justice, Fadeev
referred to Lev Gumilyov's background and suggested that "as
the son of N. Gumilyov and A. Akhmatova, he might seem to be
'useful' material for all careerists and hostile elements who might
shift their guilt to him." Fadeev also emphasized Akhmatova's
loyalty despite the campaign against her: she "conducted herself
as a good Soviet patriot and gave a decisive rebuff to all attempts of
the Western press to utilize her name."[80]

Akhmatova's situation in the late 1940's must have been unbearable. Her magnificent cycle *Requiem* is a deeply moving lament
for her imprisoned son—and for the Russian people in the grip
of the Stalinist Terror. The poet, who might at any time during the
1920's and 1930's have improved her position immeasurably by
writing according to Party dictates, would not make a public re-
cantation in 1946.

It is perhaps not surprising, however, that by 1950, after the imprisonment of Lev and the years of persecution, Akhmatova should
publish a cycle of poems under the general title *In Praise of Peace*.
Apart from Akhmatova's technical polish and infrequent oc-
currences of her most usual images, the poems might have been
done by any Party hack. Indeed, there is a possibility of a parody
of the Party-line poetry of the period. ". . . Where a tank rumbled,
there is now a peaceful tractor;/Where there was conflagration,
a garden smells sweet,/And on a road once dug up by armored
tracks/Light automobiles fly along.[81]

However drab this cycle on peaceful tractors, Pioneer camps, and
peace doves, it is hoped that Akhmatova's situation was made more
tolerable by its publication.

V *The "Thaw" and Rehabilitation*

With the exception of the five "peace" poems, Akhmatova's
original work was not printed again until the death of Stalin and
the "Thaw." Akhmatova had for a long time been interested in
the problems of literary translation, and, like many writers during
the difficult last days of the Stalin régime, she found a refuge in
translating. Her first translation during this period appeared in
the Kishinyov *Oktyabr (October)* in 1951.[82] For the next five years,
a whole series of translations followed.[83] In 1956, Akhmatova
published a translation of a whole volume of Korean classical

poetry,[84] and a number of translations from other languages.[85]

In the relaxed and relatively free intellectual atmosphere of 1956, Akhmatova's original poetry finally reappeared in *Literaturnaya Moskva (Literary Moscow)*, and a moving, bittersweet poetic autobiography, which had been written in 1945—"Memory Has Three Ages"—was included in the remarkable *Day of Poetry* in 1956.[86]

Once more, it seemed that Akhmatova was on the way toward complete rehabilitation; there were even rumors of the publication of her complete works.

It was at this time, however, that the Hungarian revolt occurred, and in the consequent tightening up, the rumors came to nothing. By August 1957, the "Thaw" was officially ended by Khrushchev's speech (printed in *Kommunist* No. 12 and reprinted in *Pravda,* August 28). Though much less violent in expression than the Zhdanov report, this speech represented, in essential points, a return to the Decision of 1946.

Perhaps because there was no desire to recall too clearly the parallel with 1946, Akhmatova was not attacked. Fadeev noted that the "patriotic and courageous conduct of a major poet of an older generation, after such a severe decision, gave rise to a deep respect for her in the literary milieu," and that Akhmatova was "made a delegate at the Second All-Union Congress of Soviet Writers."[87] The official view of Akhmatova, which had been revised around 1956, remained acceptable.[88] While Akhmatova and certain other writers, "connected in the past with decadent circles, wavered and often were mistaken in their choice of paths," they "did not betray the people."[89]

Late in 1958, a new edition of Akhmatova's poetry was published. It was the first edition since 1922. Its justification may have been in the inclusion of the "peaceful tractor" poetry of 1950, and the translations from poets of the "People's Democratic Republics," which represent about one-third of the slim volume.[90]

Poems with a recognizable erotic element, as well as those with noticeably religious themes, are omitted from the collection. The selection does not convey the predominantly sad mood of Akhmatova's poetry; the bitter and longing notes which are characteristic of her verse up to 1940 are not so much in evidence here. Also, in the book as a whole, love lyrics are disproportionately few. As might be expected, a misleading emphasis is given to the

1950 poems. Despite this lack of proportion in the selection of Akhmatova's poems, the collection is a surprisingly good one. All of the original poems are dated, and there is no attempt to distribute the 1950 poems so as to suggest their typicality. It is significant that the poem "Trenches are Dug in the Garden," singled out for attack by Egolin during the Terror, is included here. The new poems show a remarkable growth (e.g., "Prehistory," with its nostalgia for the pre-Revolutionary past, a theme unthinkable only a few years before), and there are none which are in any way similar to the 1950 cycle of "Party-line" poems. Indeed, there is a scarcely-veiled defiance of literary regimentation in a poem on Pushkin, the most potent symbol of the poet's freedom, forever violated, and rewon: "Who can say what fame is. . . ." (*Stikhotvoreniya,* p. 54). This poem seems to take an additional meaning in connection with Akhmatova's latest scholarly study of Pushkin.[91] Ironically, it was printed in *Zvezda*.

For a number of years, Akhmatova had been working on a book on Pushkin; she was particularly interested in the death of the poet and restated the question of the scholar Shchyogolev (*The Duel and Death of Pushkin*) as to why society maligned and ostracized the great poet in his last years. Akhmatova asks rather, "What did Pushkin do to them?" All the powerful of Petersburg—"swinish Petersburg," in Pushkin's words—who had attacked him, slandered him, and hated him, gradually became important only because they were his contemporaries; their names are perpetuated only because they are entered in the Pushkin archives. "They might have heard from Pushkin: 'You won't have to answer for me,/You can sleep peacefully for now./Might is right, only your children/Will curse you for my sake.'" It does not seem strained to draw the obvious parallel.

The autobiographical reference of the following quatrain, published in 1963, is indisputable: "I no longer weep for me and mine,/But if only I did not have to see on this earth/The golden brand of failure/Stamped on a still unwrinkled brow."[92]

This is an astonishingly direct plea for the artistic freedom of young Soviet poets; despite her great age and failing health, Akhmatova did not hesitate to risk her comparatively recent and presumably conditional rehabilitation. In 1964, she bravely and openly came to the defense of Iosif Brodsky, a victim of bureaucratic Philistinism. Brodsky was then an unknown and unpublished poet, whose talent Akhmatova had much admired; he was her protégé. The sentence of Brodsky for "parasitism" became a *cause célèbre* among Soviet intellectuals and shocked the Western world; the trial recalled the worst days of the Terror.[93] When Brodsky was exiled to manual labor in the far North, Akhmatova circulated a petition for his release. It was signed by leading intellectuals, among them Shostakovich, and was sent directly to Khrushchev. "Weak is my voice, but my will does not weaken" (98), Akhmatova wrote at twenty-eight in the face of personal tragedy. At seventy-five, that will remained uncompromising and strengthened by trial.

In her seventy-fifth year, Akhmatova was at last fully rehabilitated, and her entire published work—so severely criticized in the past—accepted.[94] The Western world formally recognized her poetry; in December of 1964, she travelled to Catania, Italy, where she received the Taormina Prize for Poetry. She was granted an honorary degree from Oxford and her name was being mentioned in connection with the Nobel Prize.[95] One reason it may not have been awarded is that a repetition of the Pasternak affair was feared.

Justification for a life of hardship and suffering is not in such belated recognition, but in the artistic integrity of her poetry. Her mature chefs d'oeuvre, such as *Requiem* and *Poem without a Hero*, are both sufficient justification and the ultimate vindication.

Anna Akhmatova died on March 5, 1966, at the age of seventy-seven. She was officially honored at a memorial at the House of Writers in Leningrad. By her own wish, she was laid to rest in accordance with the ancient rites of the Orthodox church. From the huge cathedral, the cortège moved to the village of Komarovo, which had been her home for the last years of her life. At her grave-side were representatives of literary organizations from all over the Soviet Union, the many admirers, the few old friends who remained, and the young poets whom she had helped and guided in her last years. They mourned the death of a superb poet, and the passing of a woman of great dignity and rectitude. They mourned also the loss of the last tie with a Russia that had been, and the last link with a great age of Russian poetry.

CHAPTER 2

Acmeism

IN the early years of her career, Anna Akhmatova was closely associated with a group of young poets who came to be known as "Acmeists";[1] however, the influence of Acmeism on Akhmatova is no longer considered to be as significant as it was at one time. For example, Akhmatova's statements concerning her longest work, *Poem without a Hero,* which was finally completed in 1962, give some indication of how far she had moved from the original Acmeist ideas.[2] Nevertheless, any study which concentrates on the first decade of the poet's creative life must give Acmeism its due as a formative influence. As late as 1961, Akhmatova thought of herself as having been an Acmeist in those early days:

In 1910, the crisis of Symbolism was clearly indicated, and beginning poets no longer joined that movement. Some went into Futurism, and others into Acmeism. I became an Acmeist.[3]

It is of course impossible to tell how much Acmeist theory affected Akhmatova's practice: critics in the 1920's tended to proceed from Acmeist principle to the analysis of Akhmatova's work, and this approach led to a certain distortion. At this point in time, it might be better simply to characterize the literary "movement" and Akhmatova's relationship to it. A later chapter of this study will consider those areas where Akhmatova's practice and Acmeist theory seem to coincide.

I *The Poets' Workshop*

"You grow kinder around young people," Alexander Blok entered in his diary one evening in 1911.[4] He had spent a "charming, casual evening" with a loosely organized group of young Petersburg intellectuals. The composition of the group was not fixed. It included, at various times, literary figures—both aspiring and arrived—members of Petersburg society, professors, critics, Bohemians, and the peasant poets who were then much in fashion. The gatherings were called "literary evenings," but had little in common with the formal, almost seminar-like atmosphere of Vyacheslav Ivanov's evenings at the Tower. The conversation was lively; there was gossip ("Who had slapped whom in Paris," as Blok's diary has it), and always the "acid humor of the literary joke" (161). Often enough there was carousing afterwards.[5]

The constant figures in this group were some dozen young people whom Gumilyov had organized into what he called the *Tsekh Poetov,* the Poets' Workshop.[6] Despite the nature of the "literary evenings," the choice of the name was not a facetious one. There were also intimate meetings of a more serious kind, sometimes at the Gumilyovs' or at the home of Sergey Gorodetsky. Gumilyov, on the subject of poetry, often took himself too seriously; his intensity communicated itself to the other members of the group. As for Akhmatova, Mme Nevedomskaya recalls, "she came alive only when the conversation was about poetry." Gorodetsky, if something of a dilettante, was at least a highly enthusiastic one. Osip Mandelstam, one of the major figures of the group, was still writing in defense of its positions as late as 1922.[7]

It is the association of such different and highly individualistic poets that literary historians call the "Acmeist school." Whether it was, indeed, "a school," in the sense of a literary group with a coherent and well-defined poetic theory, is highly doubtful. Of the two fundamental principles held by the poets in common—craftsmanship in art, and concreteness of imagery as opposed to Symbolist abstraction—the former was scarcely exclusive property of the Workshop, and the latter was not all strictly observed.

Of course, the trappings of a poetic school or movement were there: a band of young poets led by a self-proclaimed rebel against an older, established generation; a banner with a motto (in this case, "Beautiful Clarity"), a journal to rally around (the *Apollo*), manifestoes, a formal organization, a publishing venture, meetings, and studio exercises.

Nevertheless, the group was amorphous; its leader could organize but not quite convince. Gumilyov's rebellion was, in fact, without a cause, since the older generation had abandoned the positions which he attacked. The journal regularly published the works of the poets he opposed, and the editors were in any case more interested in the arts than in literature. The manifestoes were carelessly written, and published about three years after the ideas had originally been formed. The organization consisted of willful individualists who interpreted the manifestoes to suit themselves. At the meetings and studios it is quite probable that everyone learned something—perhaps a good deal—in the interchange, but it is just as probable that no one was taught anything. The formal existence of the "school," from the manifestoes in 1912 until the war which scattered its members, was barely two years.

Alexander Blok was outraged by the manifestoes and the presumption of the young people "in whose presence one grows kinder." He entered curtly in his diary: "Impressions of the last days: hatred for the Acmeists. . . ."[8] He felt that he "had to do something about the impudence of the Acmeists."[9] He prepared, eventually, a blistering attack on the fiction of a new school.[10]

Mandelstam, later himself a theoretician for the movement, in retrospect rejected the idea of a school, even though he retained the principles first expressed by Gumilyov. He observed to Irina Odoevtseva (the prominent émigrée poet who had been a student of Gumilyov's after 1918):

> It is impossible to teach anyone to write poetry. All this "poetic teaching" doesn't get anywhere. I had already been published, and successfully, when I first went to Vyacheslav Ivanov's Tower at his personal invitation. . . . Very soon, Gumilyov got hold of me. He enlightened me, revealed to me all secrets. I was even given the honor of being proclaimed an Acmeist. You know yourself what kind of Acmeist I am. But from weakness of character, I allowed a stamp to be placed on my forehead, and even tried zealously to write like an Acmeist. . . . It was difficult, very difficult, for me to free myself from his tutelage, but I managed it. . . . Gumilyov, you know yourself, is such a persuasive and natural-born teacher . . . and so loves to start literary arguments and always to be right.[11]

It is clear that "Acmeist school," "Acmeist poets," even "Acmeist principle" can serve only as convenient, if not altogether precise or descriptive labels. A recent study of Acmeism even casts doubt on the seriousness of the whole undertaking.[12] The fact remains, however, that there *was* a phenomenon which was called Acmeism, a phenomenon which is significant in the history of Russian poetry. There were major poets who called themselves Acmeists. They discussed and agreed upon certain general principles when their work was in its formative stage. Ideas current in the tenuous,

short-lived organization continued to influence the thinking of
its members in their scattered wartime isolation. These ideas
were incorporated, in one way or another, into the mature styles
of at least three outstanding poets, and thus had far-reaching
influence.

It is now rather difficult to recall—in proper perspective—the
role of Acmeism in the critical disputes of the period; the attention
since devoted to Futurism—or more specifically, to Mayakovsky—
rather obscures the issue. It is to be remembered, however, that
there was at that time a more or less even split in the Russian poetic
world, and that poets and critics declared themselves in favor of
one or the other movement.[13] Although the disputes ended arti-
ficially with Stalin's institution of the First Five-Year Plan, the
theory and example of Acmeist poets did not cease to have influence.
Gumilyov's Workshop, regenerated in 1918, was a formative experience for a number of poets who later achieved success in both
the Soviet Union and in émigré circles. An "Akhmatova style"
in Russian poetry was already so marked by 1926 that it received
mention in the *Bolshaya Sovetskaya Entsiklopediya*.

How much this influence is properly Acmeist, and how much it
is simply Akhmatova, is of course impossible to say. Indeed, even
an attempt at such a division would be mistaken. Akhmatova's
first volume, which contained essential elements of her later style,
was published well before the manifestoes and theoretical articles,
and was used to illustrate them.

As to the manifestoes themselves, despite their many short-
comings, they did at least give expression to a point of view which
had been developing for some time within the Symbolist movement.
Any pronouncement of this kind is really little more than a statement of choice or a program of action. Literary manifestoes are
bound to be partial truths with excessive claims attached to them.
The only real test was in the creative work of the Acmeists; for
this no apology is needed. It is significant that such an excellent
poet as Mandelstam should publish an article which contains the
essentials of Gumilyov's manifesto, and this some seven years
after its original publication.[14]

It would be mistaken to dismiss Acmeism as Bryusov did, as a
"hot-house plant with no roots, kept under the glass of a literary
circle's forcing bed by a few young poets who want to be original . . .
an invention, a whim, a fancy. . . ."[15]

It is similarly inadvisable to consider Akhmatova's early work as entirely separate from Acmeism, as Blok preferred to do.[16] She did not publish theoretical articles for the group, but poetic theory fascinated her, and the Workshop sessions undoubtedly helped the young poet in working out the problems of style.

In historical perspective, the poetic movement now generally accepted as Acmeism was not so much a rebellion against the reigning Symbolist school as a continuation of it—a continuation and reform. The same may be said of the Futurist movement, which burgeoned at about the same time. Broadly speaking, both new directions continued contradictory aspects of Symbolism. They defined themselves negatively by simply rejecting certain characteristics of the older movement.

Perhaps the most significant single feature of Acmeism was its rejection of the "other-world" mysticism of the Symbolists, in favor of a return to the reality of this earth.

If Romanticism may for a moment be considered the attempt in art to get away from the things of this world, and Realism, the attempt to get to the things of this world, Futurism may, again for the moment and despite the urbanistic current in it, be labeled the continuation of the Romantic aspect of Symbolism, and Acmeism, despite its exotic current, of the Realistic aspect.[17]

In the heat of their polemics, the Acmeists thought of themselves as replacing, rather than continuing Symbolism, although polite gestures were made in recognition of the debt to the older movement. Some astute critics observed the proper relation between Acmeism and the parent movement,[18] but the younger poets chose to adopt the pose of revolutionaries rather than reformers.

If there was a rebellion, it was against a kind of mystical Symbolism which was no longer characteristic of the major Symbolists, such as Blok and Vyacheslav Ivanov. When, in 1911, Ivanov pronounced his appreciation of Akhmatova's simple and unpretentious love song, it was a recognition of the changes which had come about in Russian poetry. A year earlier, Ivanov had noted what he called "new stirrings" among the Symbolists, and Blok wrote later, in his much-quoted preface to *Retribution,* "1910 is the crisis of Symbolism." In that year, both Ivanov and Blok published articles which marked the change, and suggested a plan of action which was, in essence, the program which the Acmeists were not to claim publicly until two years later.

In an address before the Petersburg Society of Devotees of the Literary Word,[19] Ivanov gave what he called "The Testament of Symbolism." It was a summation of the principles and precepts of the movement—Ivanov's view of them at least—and concluded with some interesting and quite unexpected remarks intended for the young poets of the day. Probably because of his awareness of their already perceptible dissent, he did not urge them to accept Symbolism as he had just so carefully outlined it, but advised them to go their own way. Ivanov, like Blok, was pained by the abundance of imitators and poets-by-rule who had multiplied inordinately after Symbolism had reached its apogee about 1905. "There is no need," he wrote, "to become a Symbolist"; if one should discover the Symbolist within himself, "he would do better to hide that fact from other people." Ivanov was concerned that the obligations entailed in "becoming a Symbolist" might possibly stifle young talent. He felt that even the poet who has a proper understanding of Symbolism should give more attention to his craft and not depend so much on the mystical communication of the symbol. He "must labor six days, ignoring the *realiora* (the Symbolist 'other world') so that he may reserve the seventh 'for inspiration, sweet sounds and prayers.' "[20]

In answer to Ivanov's address, Blok read a paper before the Petersburg literary society. While not a theoretician for Symbolism, Blok was unquestionably its foremost representative in practice. In concurring with Ivanov, Blok indicated even more clearly the turning point which Symbolism had reached: "the present situation of the Russian literary word clearly shows that we, the Russian Symbolists, have completed a certain part of our journey, and that we stand before new problems." In his conclusion, Blok seconded Ivanov's closing remarks and observed: "We must learn anew from the world, and from that infant who lives still in our burned-out souls."[21]

Thus, the two addresses of Ivanov and Blok contained the essentials of the Acmeist program: attention to craftsmanship in poetry and a renewed perception of the things of this world, as a child might perceive them, or in the later formulation of Gorodetsky, "like Adam at the dawn of creation."

Blok later accused Gumilyov publicly of having appropriated

the key point of the Acmeist manifesto from his address.[22] The accusation was an injustice. Gumilyov had made his position quite clear as early as 1909. In a brief review of a new volume of poems by Boris Sadovskoy, Gumilyov made a much better statement of the new, emerging ideas in Russian poetry than his manifesto later represented, and certainly a clearer expression of them than either Blok's or Ivanov's address: "Let Bryusov, like a hunter, stalk the secrets of the night, its labyrinths of passion and intellect; let Ivanov raise high the bright banner of Christ-Dionysius; let Blok long madly for his Beautiful Lady, and then scoff at her madly— Sadovskoy looks askance at all of them." It is Sadovskoy's return to an older Russian tradition, to Apollon Maykov, which Gumilyov finds refreshing after the excesses of the Symbolists. Gumilyov cites the concrete, down-to-earth imagery of Sadovskoy's poetry: ". . . the winter night, the squeak of sleigh runners, the barking of dogs, the groaning of a water-wagon. . . ."[23]

Gumilyov's review was printed in the first issue of a new literary and artistic journal, *Apollo.*[24] While it began as a new Symbolist organ, one of a long and distinguished series, the choice of name proved prophetic: it soon came to represent the opposition to the Dionysian mysteries and dark inklings of that "other world" of the Symbolists.

In 1909, when Sergey Makovsky conceived the idea of a new artistic review, he had in mind Diaghilev's *World of Art,* the most outstanding of the journals with which the Symbolists were associated. Makovsky's journal could scarcely be expected to have the revolutionary effect that *World of Art* had had some years before, or the missionary zeal of Bryusov's *The Scales.* Broadly speaking, *Apollo* merely continued the functions of the earlier journals. Makovsky intended, however, to restore attention to the arts, which had been lacking in the journals since the *World of Art.* He was himself the son of a famous painter, and had had considerable success in arranging art exhibitions.

It was at one of these exhibitions in 1909 that Makovsky chanced to meet Gumilyov, and was much impressed by him. Both were residents of Tsarskoe Selo and they soon formed a close association.[25] Gumilyov helped to gather talent for the new journal, and the young Apollonians formed the nucleus of the Poets' Workshop.

II *Forerunners*

Makovsky was looking for an older advisor for his venture into publishing, and Gumilyov suggested that he meet Innokenty Annensky. Annensky was enthusiastic about the project, and agreed to lend it his erudition and critical abilities.

Although Annensky was himself of the generation of the Symbolists, he had little enough in common with them. He was closer to the French Symbolists and the Parnassians than to any of his compatriots; while he agreed readily on the hypnotic power of the word, he had little patience with the Russian Symbolists' exaggerated claims for it. In a number of ways, his views coincided with those of the young Appollonians.

Annensky was largely ignored by his contemporaries, although his critical studies achieved some success.[26] He had published his first book of poetry, *Quiet Songs,* only in 1904. The intimacy and unassuming nature of the title indicated his difference from the impersonally philosophical and grandiloquent poetry of most Symbolists. For the first three issues of *Apollo,* Annensky wrote three long critical articles discussing the achievements and failures of the contemporary Symbolist poets.[27]

The last of the series was published posthumously. Despite his untimely death in 1909, the journal continued to be influenced by his views; indeed, among the young Apollonians, a kind of cult of Annensky developed.

Annensky's review of current Symbolist poetry was by no means negative, although he indicated clearly what had become cliché or excessive in the movement. As a critic, Annensky was remarkably objective. He was capable of passionate admiration for such different and controversial writers as Balmont and Andreev.

Annensky felt that the once-revolutionary Symbolism had lost the ability to be daring. Time had long since mellowed such incongruities as "silvering aromas" and "oleanders in ice." The reading public no longer considered them presumptuous. Further, he observed that "the modern maenad was not the same as she had been fifteen years before"; she who had been wild and ecstatic and had matured into a sober scholar: "Vyacheslav Ivanov had taught her Greek." The taste for classical antiquity among some Symbolists—nowhere, by the way, more obvious than on the pages of the early *Apollo*—had led not only to the highly productive "mythmaking," but eventually to the inclusion in poetry of classical references so obscure that even the cultured reader could not hope to comprehend them. In many cases, Annensky felt, the result was little more than a cryptogram.

Annensky was certainly not appealing for transparency in poetry; much of his own work requires a series of solutions by the reader, as though to a kind of riddle. In his poems, however, there is a poetically logical communication reinforced by, but not dependent upon, "the hypnosis of words."

While Annensky's concept of reality assumed the existence of the Symbolists' *realiora,* the "other worlds," it is with the relationship between the poet and *realia,* the things of this world, that he is principally concerned.

> *In the distinct precision of sunbeams*
> *And in the smoky confluence of visions,*
> *Over us always is the power of things*
> *With its triad of dimensions.*
>
> *And if you broaden the boundaries of life,*
> *Or multiply its forms by your fancy,*
> *There is still no escape in the* Ego *itself*
> *From the eyes of the* Non-Ego.[28]

Unlike many of his contemporaries, Annensky's "I" was not something self-sufficient or independent of the rest of the world. It was not the "I" of the priest or of a demigod, far removed from the mob.

While Annensky's lyricism is often extremely personal, he neither celebrates nor magnifies the poetic "I," and the presumption of the Symbolist-philosophers before God irritated him. In a private letter in 1909, he wrote that he would prefer a discussion with practical politicans than with Blok and the "God-seekers."[29]

Annensky's own relationship to God and immortality was ambivalent. He rejected these concepts in the name of rationality, yet he was constantly aware of a sense of "other worlds." What lay beyond death for Annensky was blankness, but his horror of a life which must end in death was real. He found escape from this ultimate reality in the world of artistic form. Georgy Chulkov called Annensky the "funereal esthete."[30]

Annensky's philosophy made him as much an outsider among the young Apollonians as he had been among the older Symbolists, but his formal views to a certain extent coincided with—and influenced—the younger poets. His influence on Akhmatova was marked; as late as 1945, she wrote in a poetic tribute to his memory "And he, whom I count my teacher,/Passed like a shade and left no shadow. . ." (5).

Although the young poets carefully nurtured their "cult of Annensky," they did not claim him as a member of the movement which was gaining impetus at the time of his death.[31]

Another poet who has been generally considered a direct precursor of the Acmeist movement is Mikhail Kuzmin. He was associated, in a certain sense, with Gumilyov's group in the early days; he was lionized in literary society and appeared at the Gumilyovs' "evenings." He also attended some of the first Workshop meetings. In his brief notes on literary prose in 1910, Kuzmin reflected the general dissatisfaction with Symbolism's theurgy, its tiresome guessing games, and mystical knowledge. He took respectful exception to the views expressed in Ivanov's "Testament," and issued an appeal for logic, comprehensibility and care in composition.

> I beg of you, be logical . . . logical in your intention as an artist, in the structure of the work, in syntax . . . be a skillful architect, both in details and the whole . . . love the word like Flaubert, be economical in means and chary of words, and you will find the secret of a wonderful thing— beautiful clarity, which I would call "Clarism."[32]

Despite the fact that Kuzmin's theoretical views seem to re-echo in the programmatic statements of the Acmeists, Akhmatova informed the present author in 1965 that he had no real influence on the group. She maintained that the identification of Kuzmin as herald to the new movement was due to a mistake made by Zhirmunsky in 1916,[33] a mistake repeated dutifully by critics ever since. Certainly, Kuzmin's own prose scarcely illustrates his theoretical statement,[34] and in any case, after 1911, his poetic talents dwindled rapidly.

Gumilyov followed Kuzmin's article in the *Apollo* with two of his own, in which he respectfully laid the Symbolist movement to rest.[35] His attitude in these articles was not altogether justifiable. He chose not to recognize the changes in the Symbolist position, although he was quite familiar with the recent ideas of Blok and Ivanov. It seems that he purposely equated the larger Symbolist movement with mystical Symbolism and lumped together the "Symbolist-esthetes" and the "Symbolist-philosophers." The "Symbolist-esthetes," since the days of the *World of Art,* had maintained a point of view similar in many ways to Gumilyov's. The artist, A. N. Benois, who had been closely associated with that journal, reflected a general tendency which had always been part of the Symbolist movement:

In our times, artists in Russia are valued for their invention, for the emotions which they provoke, rather than for the only thing that is eternal in art—for craftsmanship. I hope I live to see this situation change, and to see that the true spirit of artistic works—the form—becomes the main thing for us.[36]

It is significant that Benois' article was published in 1907, when mystical Symbolism was still widely respected, and that it appeared in *The Golden Fleece,* the organ of the extreme religious-philosophical Symbolists.

If anyone can be considered a leader in the Symbolist movement, it is Bryusov, and Bryusov chose craftsmanship over mysticism quite early in his career. He refused to consider poetry as a tool of mystical philosophy, and wrote to Blok: "Let me be a versifier only, an artist in the narrow sense of the word; the rest I leave to you . . . ."[37] Bryusov commended the efforts of Gumilyov's Workshop. In summing up its characteristics, he might have been describing his own work: attention to craftsmanship, careful choice of words, and especially "the constant checking of inspiration by intellect."[38]

Gumilyov was quite familiar with Bryusov's views; before 1910, he had been one of Bryusov's disciples. Similarly, Gumilyov was well aware of Blok's reevaluation of mystical Symbolism; the two poets were the closest during the period immediately following the founding of the *Apollo.* Further, Gumilyov need only to have read Vyacheslav Ivanov's "Testament of Symbolism" to realize that the dean of the Petersburg Symbolists no longer supported without qualification the mystical-religious branch of Symbolism.

III *The "Manifestoes"*

Despite Ivanov's "Testament," it was mystical Symbolism which Gumilyov attacked in his manifesto, which appeared in the first issue of the *Apollo* in 1913. That the article was received petulantly by Blok is scarcely surprising. While the document was significant in that it was the first relatively clear statement of the new ideas developing within the Symbolist movement, it obscured— by its revolutionary stance—the very real continuity between Symbolism and Acmeism. Gumilyov wrote:

> For the attentive reader, it is clear that Symbolism has completed its circle of development and is now declining. This is shown by the fact that Symbolist works scarcely appear any longer, and if they do appear, they are extremely weak even from the Symbolist point of view; also by the fact that more and more frequently, sonorous voices call for a review of values and reputations which were not so long ago indisputable; and also by the fact that Futurists, Ego-Futurists and other such hyenas which always follow after the lion have appeared.

> To replace Symbolism, there is a new direction, whatever it may be called—whether Acmeism (from the word *acme,* the highest degree of something, the flower, the time of flowering) or Adamism (a manfully firm view of life)—in any case, a direction requiring a greater equilibrium of powers and a more exact knowledge of the relationship between subject and object than was the case in Symbolism.[39]

D. S. Mirsky has noted that the term "Acmeism" had been used first by a hostile Symbolist; the group accepted the name in defiance. While the term can possibly be stretched to include the emphasis on craftsmanship (*acme* in the sense of "extreme sharpening"), it suggests no real innovation. Gumilyov had made clear his views in this regard four years earlier. In an essay on poetry, he maintained that poets should be guided by Coleridge, "Poetry is the best words in the best order," and Théodore de Banville, "Poetry is that which is finished, and consequently needs no reworking."[40]

The term "Adamism," on the other hand, is perhaps the better one of the two, although it has not survived. The name suggests the basic opposition to mystical Symbolism. The "Adamists" wished to see the things of this earth as themselves, not as symbols with mystical significance; in Gorodetsky's words, they wished to see things "as Adam saw them at the dawn of creation." Mandelstam later expressed his objection to Symbolism in this way:

Let us take for example the rose and the sun, a girl and a dove. There is nothing real or genuine here, only a terrible *contredanse* of "correspondences" nodding at each other. . . . Nothing wants to be itself any more. . . . A man is no longer master in his own house. . . . The household utensils have gone on strike. The broom has ceased sweeping, the pot refuses to boil, and requires the householder to contemplate its absolute significance.[41]

Gumilyov, unlike Gorodetsky, does not make the point that the term "Adamism" suggests. His definition of Adamism as a "manfully firm view of life" applies to his own poetry alone; it would seem odd if applied to the works of Mandelstam, and it is of course impossible in reference to Akhmatova. One may perhaps interpret his definition as "seeing things as they are," but his wording seems rather to suggest the aggressive and virile pose which Gumilyov assumed in his own work at this time.

"A greater equilibrium of powers and a more exact knowledge of the relationships between subject and object" is a vague and rather awkward formulation, but it does suggest the fundamental opposition to the Symbolists. The relationship between subject and object is simply the relationship between the poet and the things of this world as themselves, not as symbols and correspondences. The "greater equilibrium of powers" refers of course to restoring the balance between inspiration and the poet's craft.

Gorodetsky enlarged upon the principle of equilibrium, which Gumilyov had merely mentioned without explanation. "Art is first of all a state of equilibrium; it is solid, firm, durable." The echo of the French Parnassians here is clear. Gumilyov had translated, among other works of the French poets, Gautier's "L'Art," and the influence of Hérédia suggests itself constantly in the exoticism and love of adventure in Gumilyov's early works. While Gumilyov consciously attempted impersonality almost up to the last (and harmed his poetry in so doing), the impassivity and calm of the Parnassians did not become characteristic for the Acmeists. The emphasis on artisanry did, however, result in a related emotional restraint.

Gorodetsky theorized that not only had the Symbolists depended too much on inspiration, but that in basing themselves on the instability rather than the solidity of word meanings, they had "destroyed the royal prerogative of art—to be stable, at rest in all situations and before all critical methods."[42]

The search for stability in word meaning led the Acmeists, according to Gorodetsky, to the "living speech of the common people." They chose to return to native sources, to Pushkin and the Russian classics on one hand, and to folk poetry on the other. The folk tradition was of particular interest to Gorodetsky, and he encouraged and sponsored such outstanding folk poets as Klyuev. If Gorodetsky's folk manner was not quite successful, Akhmatova's use of folk material produced excellent results. The "concreteness" of everyday speech, if not folk speech, contributed a freshness to Acmeist poetry which had disappeared in the Symbolist preference for abstractions.

While Gumilyov valued the place of symbol in art, he would not "agree to sacrifice other poetic means to it." He sought full coordination, equilibrium in these means—the "beautiful difficulty" of Acmeism. "One of the principles of the new direction is always to take the line of most resistance."

Among the more glaring contradictions between theory and practice in Gumilyov is in his stated rejection of Symbolist views on the role of the poet. Gumilyov was never able to shed the belief that the poet is a superior being, if not precisely "priestly," then at least a leader of men and a holder of power. His words in the manifesto can be applied variously to other Acmeists, but scarcely to his own work of the period:

Man is merely a phenomenon among phenomena; we become part of the world's rhythm; we act and are acted upon. . . . For us, the hierarchy in the world of phenomena is only the specific gravity of each of them, beside which the weight of the least significant is incomparably greater than the absence of weight, of non-being, and therefore, in the face of non-being, all phenomena are brothers.

If Gumilyov scarcely saw himself as a mere "phenomenon among phenomena," these words, nevertheless, were to signal the Acmeists' plea for this earth. According to Gorodetsky, Acmeism is "a battle for this our planet Earth, vibrant, beautiful, having forms, weight, and time . . . The Acmeists' rose again became beautiful in itself, for its petals, fragrance and blossom, and not because of its supposed similarities with mystical love or whatever else." Gorodetsky continues that not only the rose is a thing of beauty, but any earthly phenomenon, even deformity. "Henceforth, *bezobrázno* (ugly) is only that which is *bezóbrazno* (without form), that which is not fully realized, that which fades somewhere between being and non-being."

Like Annensky, the Acmeists did not ignore the existence of "other worlds"; they merely found them unsuitable for poetry. Symbolism had directed its main forces into the realm of the unknowable, into mysticism, theosophy, and finally, occultism. "One may sense the unknowable," wrote Gumilyov, "but by its very definition, it cannot be known. . . ." If Gumilyov descends to some rather muddy logic in this part of his essay, his summary statement comes close to the poetic truth the Acmeists felt: "All the beauty, all the holy meaning of the stars is in this, that they are infinitely far from the earth."

In general, Gumilyov's essay seems to have been written carelessly and in haste. Revolutionary fervor could scarcely excuse it, since Gumilyov had been thinking in these terms for years, and the Workshop discussions should have resulted in a better presentation. There are some ungrammatical sentences, and at times Gumilyov assumes a completely wrong frame of reference in criticizing Symbolism. The editor of the *Apollo* observed that Gumilyov "never explained his thoughts, he 'proclaimed' them."[43] For all its faults, however, Gumilyov's essay was the more significant of the two.

Gorodetsky's essay served mainly to elaborate some of Gumilyov's formulations. While more of a piece than Gumilyov's, Gorodetsky's article was quite strained in trying to adapt Acmeist theory to works which had already been published by members of the Workshop.[44]

IV *Acmeism in Perspective*

The two manifestoes were rather strange ones to come from the pens of poets who had proclaimed Kuzmin's "Clarism," and who were followers of Annensky, who said: "The poet's first task is to think himself through." Nevertheless, they represented at long last a statement of one important direction which Russian poetry had taken after 1909.

It is perhaps worth noting briefly that Western poets during this period (and precisely during the years 1912–1913), were thinking in terms surprisingly similar to those of the Acmeists. In France, Romains and his group came to feel that "poetry over the last twenty years had lost too often contact with and even the feeling of the real"; by 1913, they had appropriated the ideas of Durtain, who was seeking *"un contrat direct: c'est à dire qu'il s'agissait d'écarter toutes les notions, toutes les données abstraites que la connaissance intellectuelle interpose, comme un écran, entre nous et les choses."*[45] If this particular group soon abandoned poetry in favor of prose and drama, others continued to concern themselves in one way or another with the problem of the relationship between object and word, with the *mot-chose,* the *poème-objet,* and the *parti pris des choses.*

It was also in 1912 that Ezra Pound arrived at some conclusions which are surprisingly similar to Gumilyov's. Considering in retrospect the faults most prevalent in poetry since 1905, he evolved these three principles:

1. Direct treatment of the "thing," whether subjective or objective.

2. To use absolutely no word that does not contribute to the presentation.

3. As regarding rhythm, to compose in the sequence of the musical phrase, not in the sequence of a metronome.[46]

It was not long after that T.S. Eliot was thinking in terms of the object and its evocative powers, and formed the idea of the objective correlative.[47]

In Russia, the Acmeists were of course not alone in redefining the nature of the poetic word; indeed, the post-Symbolist generation of poets could be characterized by their relation to it. This relation may be described in terms of a reaction against Symbolism which resulted, in various quarters, in quite different approaches to the word. There was, however, a common feature among these approaches: the conception of the word in its original, primary denotation, as opposed to Symbolist connotation and acoustical suggestion.

Mayakovsky's so-called "realization of metaphor" has the effect of recalling attention to the original sense of the word in poetry; a burning heart, for instance, is soon swarming with firemen, ladders, and hoses. Khlebnikov's "trans-sense language," apparently a destruction of the word, serves in actual fact to emphasize the primary denotations of words and word-components. The Acmeist approach, if less revolutionary, nonetheless had the same intent.

Perhaps because of the very strength of their reaction, the post-Symbolist poets—and with them the early Formalist critics—tended to identify the word with the material thing, the sign with the referent. The Formalists soon recognized the fallacy,[48] but not before another Acmeist theoretician had noted it and had expressed in a rather striking way the essentials of the later Formalist argument. Mandelstam wrote:

Do not require of poetry a doubled realness, concreteness, material nature . . . Why is it absolutely necessary to feel with the fingers? And more importantly, why identify the word with the thing, with the grass with the object it signifies?

Is the thing master of the word? . . . The living word does not signify objects, but freely chooses, as though for a habitation, one or another material significance, concreteness, a dear body. And around the thing the word roves freely, like the soul around an abandoned but not forgotten body.[49]

Mandelstam thus corrected one fallacy of the earlier manifestoes. Whatever the inherent merits or deficiencies of these articles, they were, after all, only theory; it is the practice which counts, and by this measure, no apology is needed for the works of Gumilyov, Akhmatova, and Mandelstam. Acmeism—the movement and the theory—is significant in the history of Russian poetry insofar as it was a catalyst in the literary production of these three major Russian poets.

The general principles suggested in the manifestoes affected the formative periods of these three poets, who incorporated them in various ways into their mature styles. Acmeist theory and individual style seem to have coincided most successfully in the poetry of Anna Akhmatova.

CHAPTER 3

The Love Lyrics

I *Love*

"HOW strange it is," Akhmatova wrote in 1913, "that when women—who in real life are so strong and so sensitive to all of love's enchantments—begin to write, all they know is a love which is tormenting, morbidly perceptive, and despairing."[1]

A similar generalization could have been drawn from Akhmatova's own collection *Rosary,* on which she was then working, or from her earlier published *Evening.* Perhaps it is not surprising that a poet in her early twenties should choose to sing of love, or that love's chagrin should take precedence over its charms.[2] It is, however, extraordinary that Akhmatova should devote herself almost exclusively to the subject in her more mature work as well.[3] In the four collections after *Rosary,* the love theme remains dominant despite the cataclysm of war and revolution, and the total destruction of the world that Akhmatova had known. If the tone of these volumes reflects the turmoil of the times and becomes less capricious and more austere, the focus remains inward, on a woman's ill-starred love. Recent publication of Akhmatova's poems after the long enforced silence suggests that the importance of the subject is undiminished.[4] Attitudes toward the subject change, new settings develop, and approaches vary, but it remains central throughout the six volumes. In a lovely long poem, "Memory Has Three Ages,"[5] Akhmatova effectively summarizes her attitudes toward love as they developed from *Evening* through *Anno Domini:* at first, a wary expectation of betrayal, then the bitterness of love lost, and finally, the memory of a love that once was.

In the relatively few poems built around other subjects (e.g., war, the Muse), there is often implicit the theme of a woman's love. The generalization made by Georgy Chulkov in 1915 on the basis of *Rosary* holds true through the next four collections: "there is one single theme: a strange daydream about a secret lover who had abandoned his beloved."[6]

This unusual limitation to what is effectively a single subject is not indicative of any narrowness, but of a conscious literary choice. Akhmatova's comment on the poetry of Nadezhda Lvova suggests, at least obliquely, a self-imposed limitation in the matter of poetic subject. To Boris Eykhenbaum, Akhmatova's most competent critic, the lack of variety in poetic subjects "was the result of a poetic gesture, and indicates not the nature of the poet, but a particular method."[7] In one of Akhmatova's several poems on the art of poetry, she is quite explicit about her choice of subject and poetic stance: "Never think that in delirium/And tormented by longing/I cry my misfortune loudly:/Such is my trade" (BS 156).

Despite the clarity of Akhmatova's statement in this stanza, her considered self-limitation to what is perhaps the most common lyrical subject has been misinterpreted by most of her critics. Because of the quite frequent and easily identifiable biographical details in Akhmatova's poetry, and more especially because of the parallel between Akhmatova's love for Gumilyov and the "tormenting, despairing" love in her poems, critics have rarely bothered to differentiate between the person and the *persona*. Boris Eykhenbaum's characterization of her work was a careful "something like" a continuous autobiography. His colleagues were not always so circumspect: "diary," "intimate confession," and "whispered confidences" were typical critical catchwords. When Akhmatova began her collection *The White Flock* (1916) with a poem she had composed in 1913, few people who knew her life could doubt that the lines were addressed to Nikolay Gumilyov: "And I trade in rare goods—/Your love and tenderness I sell" (BS 95).

And yet, the purely autobiographical reading does an injustice to the poet's conscious artistic choice: the single subject would then indicate a kind of monomania rather than a remarkable ability at variation.

With Emily Dickinson, Akhmatova could say, "When I state myself, as the Representative of the Verse—it does not mean—me—but a supposed person."[8] One might speak here of several "supposed persons," for the personae of Akhmatova's poems are almost as different and varied as the poems themselves.

In his book on Akhmatova, Eykhenbaum wrote: "The face of a poet in poetry is a mask."

In the image of the Akhmatova heroine, autobiographical character-istics are clearly sensed—if only because she frequently speaks of herself as a poetess. This gave rise—to an approach to Akhmatova's poetry as an intimate diary. . . . The abundance of thematic connections would seem to support the possibility of such an interpretation. But the readers of this do not see that these autobiographical references, going into the poetry, cease being personal and the further they are removed from the real interior life, the closer they come to it.[9]

Only the poet—and perhaps not even she—can make a distinct separation between herself and the "supposed person." While a purely biographical reading would ignore Akhmatova's virtuosity in treating what is effectively a single subject, it is also possible that the awareness of biographical parallels adds another dimension to the poems, thus increasing the pathos and emotional appeal rare in a poetry so highly stylized as Akhmatova's.

Before undertaking a detailed discussion of themes and subjects, it is well to subscribe to some workable definition of these difficult but inescapable terms for which the formulation of Zhirmunsky, an outstanding theoretician of poetry and an appreciative critic of Akhmatova,[10] will be used. "Each word employed by a poet is already *tema,* and through repetition can be turned into artistic motif. Each proposition is the embryo of the development of a poetic subject."[11]

For her generalization on the subject-matter of feminine lyr-icists, Akhmatova selected these lines from the poetry of Nadezhda Lvova: "O, let it be painful, tormentingly painful!/With a smile of happiness I meet all tortures./Humble, I fall prostrate in prayer/ Before the hovering phantom of parting forever." While such a direct and passionate statement approaches bathos in Lvova's immature treatment, the quatrain nevertheless contains not only Akhmatova's predominating view of profane love as pain and betrayal, but also characteristic secondary motifs which are rep-resented here by religious imagery, the suggestion of martyrdom, and the pose of humility and resignation. The paradox of these lines receives a vastly more effective treatment in Akhmatova's version: "Glory to thee, pain without egress!/The grey-eyed king died yes-terday."[12]

Here, in a typically laconic manner, Akhmatova manages to

compress the paradox into a single line—and, with typical restraint, casts the sentiment in the basically impersonal nature of a highly stylized ballad.

There were many Russian poets who attempted to imitate Akhmatova in manner, but very few were successful. Most did not even reach the modest level of Nadezhda Lvova.

> . . . (Akhmatova's) love became . . . a corvee, a martyrdom. Young ladies, sweet provincial poetesses, diligently imitating Akhmatova, did not understand the significance of the lines at her bitterly pressed lips. They tried to take the measure of the dark shawl, slipping from the slightly bent shoulders, unaware that they were measuring a cross.[13]

For Akhmatova, love was "morbidly perceptive"—the "hovering phantom" pervades the whole of the first published collection *Evening* (1912), which was written during the period when her marriage was at its happiest. In this volume, like those which follow, love presumes loss or betrayal. Love is "an aerial thing and momentary" (V 230); "love conquers deceitfully" (V 227); it is a "deceitful land where lovers wander and regret" (V 240); love "is a poisoner" (V 228).

It is interesting to note that even in Akhmatova's very earliest work (two poems from the first copy book), desertion and abandonment provide the setting. One of these begins with a lovers' quarrel:

> *Neither of us yet understood*
> *How small the earth is for two people.*
> *And that memory infuriated tortures you,*
> *That the trial of the strong is a fiery*
> *   sickness,*
> *And that in the bottomless night the*
> *   heart teaches us*
> *To ask: oh, where is my beloved gone? . . .*[14]

If the subject was already prominent in Akhmatova's earliest poetry, the manner of treating it gradually moved toward the careful understatement we now consider characteristic of her verse. Compare, for example, the poem "Love," written in 1911:

> *Now like a little snake, coiled,*
> *It casts its spells near the very heart,*

> *Now for days on end, like a dove,*
> *It coos on the white window sill.*
>
> *Now it gleams in bright hoarfrost,*
> *Now seems to appear in the slumber of*
>   *flowering stock . . .*
> *But surely and secretly it leads away*
> *From joy and from peace.*
>
> *It can sob so sweetly*
> *In the prayer of a yearning violin,*
> *But it is frightful to discern it*
> *In a smile still unfamiliar.* (V 223)

In the collections following *Evening*, love's deceitfulness remains a constant. "In love's every word there is betrayal (AD 48); "the Lord granted not that the heart should live without deceit" (BS 168); love is a thief (Ch 178); and only in dreams does a lover not confuse the name of his beloved with that of another (P 90).

Love is pain; a sharp needle in the breast (Ch 183)—a ring on the third finger is the sting of a wasp (V 235). Prayer cannot relieve the torment; love sucks up the soul as through a straw (V 234); it is a pain which only a voiceless nightingale can know (Ch 206). Love is trial by iron and fire (P 75); it is the way of the cross (AD 49). Love is imprisonment (BS 131), captivity (Ch 182); its nets are strong (Ch 187) and its chains heavy. Love is the fifth season, where freedom breathes its last—but it alone is worthy of praise (BS 149). Love is a wearying, debilitating, suffocating illness. The body is strangely weak (V 244, 226); trysts are wearying (Ch 210), and even love's happiness is wearisome and tiring (Ch 164). The flesh wearies in a grievous illness (BS 103); a hand grown weak cannot raise itself to wipe a tear (BS 137); the knees weaken against the will (BS 124). Love's happiness suffocates (P 70); so does its grief (AD 44).[15]

Removed from context, these references would seem to suggest a poetry rather wearying and suffocating in itself. The very frequency of the *tema,* however, indicates Akhmatova's ingenuity in variation rather than over-repetition. The variety in statement of the single motif represents in itself a technical tour de force.

In the later volumes, the motif of tragic love escapes over-sentimentality in its expression through an almost calm, epic resignation before suffering. In the earliest work, however, the *persona* is more often unreconciled to love's pain, and the lyrical statement

lacks the indirection characteristic for more restrained works
of the later period. This poem, for example, was written in 1911:

> I wept and I repented,
> If only the skies would thunder!
> My dark heart was drained
> In your inhospitable* house.
> The pain I know is unendurable,
> The shame of the road back.
> How awful to go back to the unloved one,
> The unloved one who is quiet and humble.
> I will bend to him in my finery,
> My necklaces tinkling;
> He will ask only: "My beauty!
> Where have you been praying for me?" (V 254)

The first half of this poem is a quite direct expression of lyrical
emotion, yet even in this early work there is already evidence of a
peculiar device which later becomes typical and which lends an
odd kind of objectivity to the expression. By this device, the *persona*
of the poem is displaced, as though she stands apart from herself,
observing herself in suffering.[16] In the example at hand, the shift
is from direct address to the description of a dramatic scene in which
the *persona* is a player.

While the depth of the emotion in this example is indicated
directly in the first half of the poem, the precise nature and full force
of the emotion is not established until the last lines. At mid-point,
there is a shift from the first-person statement to a grammatically
impersonal construction, and there follows the highly condensed
dramatic scene, complete with gestures, speech, and minor detail.

The emotional force of the poem derives not from the initial statement, but from the imagined charade at the end. The last lines
establish the lyrical emotion as remorse after betrayal. It is clearly
suggested that the deception was calculated, and that the occasion
for finery was given as church, although the real reason was an assignation. The pain of continuing the deception becomes acute as
the *persona* pictures the return home, the forced hypocritical gesture
of tenderness, the tinkling necklace mocking her hypocrisy, and

---

* *Nezhiloy* means both uninhabited and uninhabitable; the play on the ambiguity
here is interesting with regard to the secondary motif of homelessness which is to be
discussed below. An uninhabited house signifies love lost, and an uninhabitable
house—that is, one which cannot be lived in, suggests rejection.

the innocent question of "the quiet one" which will recall the full enormity of the deception.

In another poem from *Evening,* there is no direct statement of lyrical emotion at all: there is the suggestion of an interior, and then a kind of conversation between the *persona* and herself.

Here, the *tema* is not deception, but abandonment. It is established in the first four lines simply through a progression of concrete objects:

> *The door is ajar,*
> *The lindens rustle sweetly . . .*
> *On the table forgotten*
> *Are a riding crop and glove.*
>
> *The circle from the lamp is yellow . . .*
> *I listen to the rustling.*
> *Why did you go away?*
> *I don't understand.*
>
> *Joyous and clear*
> *Will the morning be tomorrow.*
> *Life is splendid,*
> *Heart, be wise.*
>
> *You're quite tired,*
> *You beat more quietly, hollowly.*
> *You know, I was reading*
> *That souls are immortal.* (V 231)

The first person occurs only in the second stanza, but it scarcely gives direct expression to the pain of abandonment. The question which restates the *tema* ("Why did you go away?") is not an anguished cry from the heart, but a question posed in stunned puzzlement. The first person statement shifts to second person address. The pathos of the situation is in the attempt of the *persona* to console her heart with promises which are now pointless.

The shift from direct lyrical expression to a more indirect method was to develop in some later poems to the almost complete suppression of the lyrical "I," to the almost complete detachment of the *persona* from herself. The following poem is from *Rosary,* and the first person is entirely avoided. As in the preceding example, the poem opens with a suggestion of an interior through a succession of not particularly related concrete objects. An address in the second person follows abruptly; the identity of the person addressed is not immediately clear, nor, indeed, is the identity of the speaker. The final stanza returns to impersonal construction and finally to the ordinary third person.

> Under the ikon, a frayed rug,
> It is dark in the cool room,
> And the thick, dark-green ivy
> Winding, has covered over the wide window.
>
> From roses streams a sweet scent,
> The ikon light crackles, scarcely burning.
> The linen chests have been painted brightly
> By the loving hand of a village artisan.
>
> And at the window, an embroidery frame
>   shines white . . .
> Your profile is delicate and severe.
> You hide your kissed fingers squeamishly
> Under your kerchief.
>
> And for your heart to beat is frightful,
> There is such mournfulness in it now . . .
> And in your rumpled braids is hidden
> The scarcely sensed smell of tobacco smoke. (Ch 214)

Here, the major motif of love as pain is represented by the *tema* of seduction, presumably followed by rejection. It is the final lines, once again, which give the key to interpretation of the poem, and the identification of the second person as the *persona* herself. The catalogue of details of the interior stops abruptly in the third stanza, almost as though the *persona* may have caught a glimpse of herself in a mirror. The apparently distracted apprehension of the details of the room is replaced by a rush of recollection; the "kissed fingers" are hidden beneath a kerchief. The *tema* is revealed at last, delicately and obliquely, through the barely perceptible scent of tobacco smoke lingering in the "rumpled braids."

The curious thing about the three examples cited above is not, of course, that lyrical expression should be in persons other than the first. It is the stance or point of view of the *persona*—somehow apart from herself, observing herself—which is most unusual. The peculiar stance permits an emotional distance, a degree of restraint and a certain objectivity in the expression of intense lyrical emotion. This device, with its shifts in grammatical person and the unusually infrequent use of the first person, is one of the principal reasons that Akhmatova's almost exclusive treatment of the difficult subject of love's pain avoids any impression of mawkishness.

The poems cited above are typical for the variety of ways in which the device is used: direct lyrical statement may be combined with the description of a dramatic scene in which the *persona* is a figure; the description of an interior may serve both to state the *tema* and to provide a setting in which the persona observes herself; in another setting, she may stand entirely apart.

Variety in approach to the subject is also indicated by the three poems. It is treated here, for example, in three different aspects: betrayal, abandonment, seduction and rejection. Accordingly, the personae are themselves quite different in character. One, a wordly and calculating, if remorseful, deceiver; the second is a woman once loved and now cast aside, stunned by her loss; the third, a young woman facing herself after seduction.

The persona of the first poem is somewhat atypical; almost always, the woman is cast as the aggrieved party.[17] Practically all the poems are written from a woman's point of view; the number of instances where Akhmatova speaks in the masculine gender is insignificant.[18]

The thoughtful scholar and critic N.V. Nedobrovo [to whom, incidentally, Akhmatova dedicated the poem "Statue at Tsarskoe Selo" (BS 128)] observed that Akhmatova can be most correctly described by the term "woman-poet," with the accent on the first word.[19]

II *Details*

To some extent, it is the sensitivity to furnishings and décor, and certainly the attention to details of feminine attire and coiffure which reminds us constantly that it is a woman who is speaking in Akhmatova's poetry. It would be mistaken, however, to interpret the prominence of such details simply as a preoccupation with traditionally feminine concerns. These necklaces and embroidery frames, painted chests and scarves are the materials from which Akhmatova's poems are constructed, and reflected the Acmeist love of concrete things. Akhmatova is highly selective in her choice

of concrete objects, and items of dress and décor are two categories
on which she typically draws. They occur so frequently that they
present in themselves minor motifs.

Some of Akhmatova's best-known poems turn precisely on details
of attire. The famous "Song of the Last Meeting" effectively conveys
the shock and confusion of the *persona* by the drawing of a left-hand
glove onto the right. Gloves (I 30), veils (V 228), kerchiefs (Ch 204),
muffs (Ch 230) are typical items; a gown of white silk (AD 56)
and a grey housedress (Ch 203), white dancing slippers (Ch 180)
and shoes with run-down heels (Ch 203) mark contrasts in moods.
The impersonality of garden statuary disappears when the poet
notes in passing that a statue is "elegantly coiffed" (BS 120). Un-
curled bangs (P 89), braids plaited tightly for the night (Ch 205) or
wound round the head for swimming (Ch 199) add an extremely
feminine intimacy to a poetry which, in its form and syntax, generally
strives toward the impersonal. One poem, for example, manages
to achieve a highly personal note, even though words indicating
the first person are kept to a minimum. Again, the effect is that of
the *persona* watching herself suffer.

> *Around the neck a string of tiny beads,*
> *In the wide muff, I hide [my] hands,*
> *The eyes look distractedly about*
> *And will never weep again.*
>
> *And the face seems paler*
> *From the lilac-colored silk ;*
> *My uncurled bangs*
> *Reach almost to the brows.*
>
> *And not similar to flight*
> *Is this slow gait,*
> *As though there were a raft beneath [my] feet,*
> *And not the little squares of the parquet.*
>
> *And the pale lips are slightly opened,*
> *Uneven the difficult breathing,*
> *And on my breast tremble*
> *The flowers of a meeting that never was.* (P 89)

In order to convey the suppression of the first person pronouns
in the Russian, the above translation is necessarily awkward.

The omission of possessive pronouns is, of course, quite permissible and not at all extraordinary in Russian. The fact that they are so often omitted here is, however, unusual.

While this poem draws heavily on the category of feminine attire for its imagery, it is the single, unexpected details of the little squares of parquet which is employed to suggest the intense pain of the moment. It is in just such rapid focusing on concrete detail that Akhmatova's practice and Acmeist theory most effectively coincide. Given this focus, ordinary objects are "perceived anew," are evoked in their solidity, their texture, their mass. While they serve to communicate emotions which are often quite unrelated to them, they are not symbolic, but remain themselves, the Acmeist "things."

The most common household objects—although unusual ones in poetry, appear in extraordinary juxtapositions. Sunmotes on a corroded sink console the abandoned heroine; roses in a washstand pitcher (AD 62) convey an impression of extreme intimacy; a cast-iron fence and a pine bed (AD 51) begin a poem expressing the heroine's resigned acceptance of abandonment. There is a profusion of beds, tables, chairs, even a motley hammock appears; a pillowcase embroidered with an owl, a high pier-glass. Akhmatova's poetry is in more than one sense "a poetry of the intérieur."[20] The poems are set for the most part within the house (and the garden wall the outermost limit); often there is a specific location within a particular room: entrance hall or bedroom, parlor or dining room.[21] The effect of such settings is to create an atmosphere of intimacy, as well as to suggest a specific, concrete background for the brief and rapidly developed dramatic scenes. With the Acmeist fondness for the concrete, Akhmatova includes minor details of the rooms, and the physical setting is often fixed in time as well as place. All this is done with a maximum verbal economy.

> *Do you want to know how it all happened?*
> *It had just struck three in the dining room,*
> *And saying goodbye, lingering at the thresholds,*
> *She said as though with difficulty:*
> *"That is all . . . Oh, no, I forgot,*
> *I love you, I loved you*
> *Even then."*
> *—"Yes." (V 232)*

Within the space of eight lines, Akhmatova manages to convey the suggestion of a quiet house, the quiet intensified by the awkward silences of a difficult leavetaking, the tentative hesitancy of a woman, as she passes through a succession of rooms, clinging to the moment of parting, and finally, the coolness and reserve of her now indifferent lover.[22]

III *The House*

Given the frequency of rooms and interiors in Akhmatova's poetry, it is perhaps not surprising that "house" should be one of the commonest words in her lexicon. There is a reflection here of the Acmeist fondness for architectonic imagery, but the house has a more complex function than merely providing concrete background. The house is also symbolic, on this level intimately related to the major motif. One of the aspects in which Akhmatova sees tragic love, for example, is as imprisonment; the house without love is a prison: *"Ya ne khochu ni trepeta, ni boli,/Mne muzh palach, a dom ego—tyur'ma"* ("I do not want pain, nor to tremble,/My husband is a hangman, and his house a prison") (AD 65). The heroine is a "sad captive" (V 241), she lives in the house "wingless and tamed" (I 13), "like a cuckoo in a clock" (V 235).[23]

If the major motif is often represented by the *tema* of imprisonment, it is much more frequently conceived in terms of abandonment. Quite often, the motif is stated through imagery of the house. The abandoned house signifies the abandoned heart: *"Pod kryshey promyorzshey pustogo zhil'ya/Ya myortvennykh dney ne shchitayu"* ("Under the frozen roof of the empty house/I do not count the deadening days") (BS 113); *"I na stupen'ki vstretit'/Ne vyshli s fonaryom./V nevernom lunnom svete/Voshla ya v tikhy dom"* ("And no one came out on the steps/To meet me with a light./In the treacherous moonlight/I entered the silent house") (Ch 180). *"Ya davno predchuvstvovala etot/Svetly den' i opustely dom"* ("Long since have I had a foreboding of this/Bright day and abandoned house") (I 27).

If the details of the interiors are specific, those of the house are the simplest, most general ones: a roof and some steps occur typically in the excerpts cited above, and the most frequent details are doors and windows. These occur for the most part without any description or qualifying adjectives. On the symbolic level, doors and windows are conceived in their original sense; the door as ingress or barrier; the window as an opening or eye.[24] These simple symbolic conventions are often used to convey the lyrical sentiment. To express hopeless yearning and yet hopeful expectation, for example: *"Akh, dver' ne zapirala ya/ Ne zazhigala svech"* ("Oh, I did not lock the door; I did not light the candles"—the poem ends "I was sure that you'd return") (V 244). To express a woman's complete submission: *"Ya okoshka ne zavesila,/ Pryamo v gornitsu glyadi"* ("I did not curtain the window/Look right into my chamber") (P 82). Longing is conveyed by this familiar image: *"Dlya tebya v okoshke stvorchatom/Ya vsyu noch sizhu s ognyom"* ("I sit all night with a candle/In my casement window for you") (V 241); here, the otherwise trite image is effective because the stylized setting appears to be the house of a peasant. A shuttered window signifies the impossibility of seeing the beloved: *" V dome u dorogi neproezzhey/Nado rano stavni zapirat'"* ("In the house by the impassable road/The shutters must be locked early") (Ch 198).

The door (gate, doorsill, threshold) is an entrance for love or a barrier against it. It marks a boundary between joy and despair; it signifies reunion, or more often, abandonment. The image of the threshold figures prominently in the expression of final parting; doorsills and gates mark rejection by the lover (V 228, Ch 204, P 69, Ch 197); less frequently, the door is open to love (AD 58, V 244).

The following poem, which is in many ways typical of Akhmatova's treatment of the love theme, makes use of the image of a gate to suggest a barrier to love.

> *I wrung my hands beneath the dark veil . . .*
> *"Why are you so pale today?"*
> *—Because I gave him of bitter sadness*
> *To drink, until he was drunk with it.*
>
> *How shall I forget? He went out, stumbling,*
> *His mouth twisted awry with pain. . . .*
> *I ran, not touching the doorsills,*
> *Ran after him as far as the gate.*
>
> *Out of breath, I shouted: "It was all a joke,*
> *What happened. If you go, I shall die."*
> *He smiled calmly and terribly*
> *And said to me: "Don't stand in the wind." (V 228)*

This poem, which is incidentally one of Akhmatova's most famous, incorporates a number of the typical devices discussed above. There is the detail of feminine dress, and the poem is a particularly interesting example of the ambiguity of grammatical person. In the Russian, the person in the first line is indeterminate; only the feminine gender is indicated. The speaker in the second line is entirely unidentified; it may be someone not involved in the drama later described, or possibly, once again, the *persona* addressing herself, as though in a mirror. Only after the third line is the ambiguity resolved. The description of a quickly developed, intense dramatic scene follows: it reaches a breaking point of emotion in the last line with the calm finality of the lover's words. The function of the doorsills in this poem is quite similar to that in the last complete poem cited: in both cases, they are associated with an imminent, probably permanent parting.

This short poem, perhaps as well as any other, illustrates Akhmatova's approach to the almost exclusive subject of love: the only love which she felt women could sing, a love "tormenting . . . and despairing." Here is the cruel capriciousness of love, the torment it brings, and ultimately, the despair of love irrevocably lost.

In considering the poems and excerpts cited in the preceding pages, it is interesting to note the quite different functions of the rooms and interiors as opposed to the house as it is used in Akhmatova's treatment of the major subject. If the interiors are specific and detailed, providing background, the house itself is conceived in general terms, almost archetypal, and it has a symbolic function. If the interiors lend a certain intimacy to Akhmatova's love lyrics, the house and its generalized details do not all have this effect. Note, for example, the following poem, in which the symbolism of the house is employed, and which is closer in nature to epic song than love lyric:

Lot's Wife

And the righteous man followed the emissary of God,
Great and shining over the black mountain.
But alarm spoke loudly to the wife—
It is not late, you can still look back

At the red towers of your native Sodom,
At the square where you sang, at the court
    where you spun,
At the blank windows of the high house
Where you bore children to your dear husband.

> *She looked, and fixed by deadly pain,*
> *Her eyes could look no more;*
> *And her body turned into transparent salt,*
> *And her swift feet* were rooted to the ground.*

> *Who will weep for this woman?*
> *Is she not deemed the least of all losses?*
> *My heart at least will never forget*
> *The one who gave her life for a single*
>   *glance back.* (I 22)

The image of the house is central. Once again, there is the suggestion of windows as eyes; without being personified exactly, the house seems somehow bereft as Lot's wife looks back on the blank windows. Here, the imagery of the house is connected only tangentially with the major motif; the deserted house symbolizes not just loss of love, but ultimate tragedy. The idea of homelessness, of leaving home to wander, is in itself an important motif in Akhmatova's poetry; it will be discussed in detail below. There are, however, two other motifs which are represented obliquely in this extraordinary free variation on the Biblical theme.

If we remember that this poem was written just after Gumilyov's death, at a time when many Russian intellectuals were leaving Russia, and that Akhmatova categorically refused to leave her homeland, there is a possibility of a dual interpretation. There is in the poem a quite clear parallel with Akhmatova's choice to remain in her beloved Petersburg, despite the dangers and intolerable difficulties involved. The parallel to the emigration suggests inevitably the revolution. Petersburg and Russia at war are important secondary motifs in Akhmatova's poems, and are often inseparable. Both motifs exist in a close, complex relationship to the pervasive major motif of tragic love.

---

* The epithet here is fixed; it is from Russian folk poetry. This poem appeared first in 1940, but judging from a clear reference to it in a poem by Pasternak in 1928, it was presumably written 1922–23. "Anna Axmatova," *Stixi i poemy* 1912–32 (Ann Arbor: University of Michigan Press, 1961).

CHAPTER 4

The Themes of War and of the City

I War

ALTHOUGH contemporary concerns did not ordinarily penetrate the intimate world of Akhmatova's lyrics, the threat to her homeland struck deep into her poetic consciousness; she produced a small number of highly moving poems concerning Russia during World War I, and later, in revolution.

The general regard in which these poems are held (they are among the most frequently reprinted) testifies to their effectiveness, but Russian critics have tended to give them disproportionate attention in terms of the total number of poems in any single volume, and to create an exaggerated impression of their typicality. Mochulsky, for example, wrote of *The White Flock:* "The poet has left behind the circle of intimate experiences, the coziness of her 'dark blue' room, and the circle of recherché emotions and capricious refrains" in favor of the themes of the motherland and of the war.[1] Another reviewer wrote that "both the war and the revolution scorched her face, but we are told not about the conflagration itself, but about how the flames licked each object, each day of the present."[2]

In actual fact, only five poems from the total of selections in *The White Flock, The Plantain,* and *Anno Domini* could be said to be "about" war and revolution. Of these, only three ignore the love motif entirely. One poem fuses the love motif into a complex unity with the motifs of war and Petersburg. Passing impressions of soldiers returning from parade in 1914 register on the consciousness of the heroine as she wanders distracted through the streets of the city. Her mind is in turmoil; lost love is implicit. She searches through a January snowstorm for her lost love, symbolized characteristically by "an almost white house" with a sunporch and a sloping roof. Someone had removed the house, spirited it away to "foreign cities"; no one seems to notice that it is gone.

The almost white house represents the past, as well as past love; it is a whole way of life soon to be swept away in a great storm. The "light anxiety" of January 1914 is reflected in the carefully maintained whimsical mood of the poem, providing a contrast to the starkness of the prophecy. Both the tragedy of love lost and the frightful prospect of Russia at war are bound up in the single symbol of the "almost white house" lost in a snowstorm.

> *A frosty sun. From parade*
> *The soldiers come on and on.*
> *I'm glad of this January noon,*
> *And my anxiety is light.*
>
> *I remember each twig here,*
> *And each silhouette.*
> *Through the white gauze of hoarfrost*
> *Drips a crimson light.*
>
> *There was an almost white house here,*
> *A glassed-in porch.*
> *How many times with a wooden, hesitant hand*
> *I held the bell-pull.*
>
> *How many times . . . Play soldiers,*
> *And I'll look for my house,*
> *I'll know it by its sloping roof,*
> *By its eternal ivy.*
>
> *But somebody moved it,*
> *Took it away to foreign cities*
> *Or has taken from my memory*
> *Forever the way to it.*
>
> *The bagpipes die away in the distance,*
> *The snow flies like cherry blossoms . . .*
> *And apparently no one knows*
> *That the white house is gone.* (BS 152)

The "light anxiety" and fantasy of this poem gives way to a sterner statement in "To the Memory of July 19, 1914," from which this stanza is taken: "From memory, like a weight henceforth superfluous,/Have disappeared the shadows of songs and passions./ Now empty, it has been ordered by the Almighty/To become the terrible book of tidings of storm" (BS 148).

Despite the poetic hyperbole of the first two lines, only two further poems in the entire collection abandon "the shadows of songs and passions." One is a woman's prayer in time of war (BS 137), and the other, "July 1914," is a two-part poem, rich in the images of Akhmatova's homeland, solemn and severe in its evocation of national cultural traditions. Here is the first part:

> It smells of burning. Four weeks
> Has the dry turf burned in the swamps.
> Even the birds did not sing today,
> And the aspen leaves no longer quiver.

> The sun became God's punishment,
> The rain has not sprinkled the fields
>   since Easter.
> There came a one-legged passer-by
> And alone in the yard, he said:

> "Terrible times are nearing. Soon
> It will become crowded with fresh graves.
> Expect famine, and earthquakes and plague
> And eclipse of the heavenly luminaries.

> Only the enemy shall not divide
> Our land for his pleasure:
> The Holy Virgin will spread a
>   white cloth
> Over great sorrows." (BS 135)

The note of prophecy sounded here is an interesting minor *tema*. It seconds the prophetic snowstorm in the example preceding, and in the only other poem dealing specifically with war and revolution, it is notably prominent. The poem is perhaps the best known of the war poems of this period: "Everything is plundered, betrayed, sold off."

It is Akhmatova the Acmeist who prophesies here in a way distinctly reminiscent of the Symbolist poets. The last stanza reads: "And so close something marvellous comes/To the ruined, dirty houses,/Something known to no one, to no one,/But desired by us for all ages" (AD 47).

It is the sterner poetic person whose "lips no longer kiss, but prophesy" (BS 156); she has foresight (BS 105); she has secret knowledge of the future (AD 61). It is with respect to the role of the seer for the *persona,* especially in connection with war and Revolution, that one of the few positive comparisons can be made with the Symbolist Blok and the Futurist Mayakovsky.

The austere, solemn poetic person of the war poems, and those which forcefully reject the emigration (P 91 and AD 41),[3] are not typical for the war period. The poems which have war, Revolution, and emigration as their subjects number not more than seven or eight in the three wartime volumes taken together. National themes are secondary to the love motif; sometimes, as we have seen above, they are congruent (BS 152). The same superposition of motifs occurs in another poem from *The White Flock.* Here, peace is represented by a young girl, in some far country where there is no war, talking quietly over the fence to her neighbor at evening, and "only the bees overhear the tenderest of all possible conversations." This imagined scene is contrasted to the "solemn and difficult life" of Petersburg:

> *But not for anything would we exchange*
> *the sumptuous*
> *Granite city of glory and of woe,*
> *The glittering ice floes of the wide rivers,*
> *The sunless, somber gardens*
> *And the voice of the Muse barely heard.* (BS 122)

There is here only an oblique suggestion of war in the words "solemn and difficult life," and in the recognition that the "sumptuous granite city" might conceivably be lost to the enemy. It is, nevertheless, Akhmatova's Petersburg which is the central focus of this poem rather than the prospect of war. If the two motifs are often connected, it is the motif of Petersburg which is by far the more pervasive in Akhmatova's poetry during these years.

II *The City*

Among the great cities of the world, there are a number which seem to be especially rich in history and tradition, in grandeur and beauty, in atmosphere and mood. Petersburg is one of these cities, and it is in this sense like Paris or Venice, London or Vienna. Such cities possess a certain power of evocation; the petrified past seems at one with the living present.

Petersburg has worked its spell on a number of distinguished Russian literary figures. The eighteenth century court poets sang its splendors in solemn odes; Pushkin recreated in verse both its imperial magnificence and its sinister malevolence; Gogol lent his grotesque vision to its description, and Dostoevsky probed the dark corners of this "most intentional city in the world." For the Symbolists, urban themes were characteristic, and Petersburg was a favorite subject for their "myth-making."

In Akhmatova's poetry, one is constantly reminded of the city she calls "the murkiest of capitals." Fragmentary views of the city seem to register involuntarily in the mind of the preoccupied poetic person. In many poems, there is apparently a subconscious awareness of Petersburg: there are glimpses of classical architectural line, the patterned shadows of the city's wrought-iron fences, the altar wall of St. Catherine's Church, a sky-blue mansard on one of the islands in the Neva, the dome of St. Isaac's Cathedral arrayed in silver. Such perspectives appear repeatedly, momentarily in Akhmatova's poems. She knows the magnificence of Petersburg's "sumptuous military reviews," of its monuments and its palaces. She knows also the life and the contemporary reality of the great city: steam rises in winter from yellow livery stables; the odor of hemp and tar from mooring hawsers is sharp; there is the clatter of traffic on resounding bridges, and smoke swirls down from blackened factory chimneys. Akhmatova is sensible also to the mystique of the granite city "above the dark-watered Neva, under the cold smile of Emperor Peter" (V 209). Such adjectives as "murky" (*mrachny:* BS 127), "gloomy" (*ugryumy:* BS 153), and "severe" (*strogy:* BS 121), and "frightening" (*strashny:* BS 147) reflect one aspect of what has come to be called the "Petersburg myth." In another aspect, the city is "wonderful" *(divny:* BS 167), "marvellous" (*chudesny:* BS 105); these last two words, weak in English, have retained somewhat more of their original sense in Russian. While these epithets would not be out of place in the lexicons of Akhmatova's Symbolist contemporaries and predecessors, her images tend toward the concrete rather than the chimeric.

Akhmatova's attitude toward the city is, on the one hand, traditional: the mystique of the city permeates her poems, and grandeur past and present is frequently evoked. On the other hand, the attitude is familiar and proprietary. These attitudes are of course not mutually exclusive, and their juxtaposition in Akhmatova's poetry can be singularly effective:

> *You were my blessed cradle*
> *Dark city on the menacing river,*
> *And my triumphant wedding bed,*
> *Over which your young seraphim*
> *Held our wedding crowns,*
> *City, loved by me with a bitter love.*
>
> *Prie-dieu* of my prayers*
> *Were you, stern, silent, misty.*
> *There first appeared to me my beloved,*
> *Who showed me my shining path,*
> *And there my sad muse*
> *Led me like a blind woman.* (BS 111)

Here, while the Petersburg of literary tradition is clearly suggested, personal motifs characteristic for Akhmatova—motifs of love, religion, the Muse—are practically predominant. Still, this is the only poem in the five volumes which can be said to have Petersburg as the poetic subject. It is interesting to note that the two-part poem entitled "Verses About Petersburg" (Ch 209) has essentially for poetic subject a remembrance of past love.[4]

In some twenty-odd poems in which Petersburg is given a prominent role, the city functions not as a focus, but as a background for the love motif, as a backdrop for the drama. A bench in the Catherine Garden is a place to remember lost love (P 84); two lovers in a small boat slip by the white columns of the Senate in the night (BS 125); the Winter Palace and the fortress of Saints Peter and Paul are a background for a lovers' quarrel on a bridge over the Neva (Ch 188).

The point of view, carefully maintained, is that of a woman in love; Petersburg is perceived through her eyes:

> *God's angel, who on a winter morning*
> *Secretly betrothed us,*
> *Will not take his darkened eyes*
> *From our life which has no sadness.*
>
> *This is why we love the sky,*
> *The thin air, the fresh wind*
> *And the branches growing black*
> *Beyond the wrought-iron fence.*

---

* *soleya* means a long, narrow platform or sill in front of an iconostasis, on which one may kneel for prayer when the Divine Liturgy is not being sung.

This is why we love the stern,
Watery, dark city,
And why we love our partings
And the hours of our brief meetings. (BS 121)

Often, when the city is not employed as background, it is nevertheless present in the consciousness of the poetic person. To express
the thought "how can you go on living, not knowing of my love,"
the poetic person asks simply: "How can you look at the Neva,/
How can you go onto the bridges?" (BS 113).

In a poem without a specifically urban setting, the consciousness
of the watery city emerges without any direct references to it.
The heroine, pleading not to be rejected by her lover, says: "It is
light and simple here in your room,/Don't make me go there/Where
under the stifling vault of the bridge/The dirty water grows cold"
(Ch 189).

The suggestion of suicide here recalls the city in its threatening
and sinister aspect. Pushkin had established this aspect of Petersburg
and it was elaborated by both prose writers and poets of the nineteenth century. It was further developed by the Symbolists' interest
in what Baudelaire had called *"le paysage des grandes villes,"*
which included the viciousness, perverseness, and decadence of
urban life. The ugliness and depravity of modernity fascinated the
Symbolists, who moved beyond the Russian Naturalists' description
of the "physiology" of the city to its irreality, its deceitful illusion.

For Bely and Bryusov and Balmont, the city was a phantasm;
Blok, moving from the social and cultural complexities of the
city in the manner of Verhaeren, came under the spell of the night
city with its decadence, cabarets and *cafés chantants*. His concrete
details are lost in a maze of chimeric allusions.

While there are some points for comparison between Akhmatova and the Symbolist poets with regard to urban themes, there
is a fundamental difference in attitudes. Where the city is secondary
to the dominant motif of love in Akhmatova's poetry, it is often
the poetic subject for the Symbolists. If the city is illusory in Symbolist poetry, it is concrete in Akhmatova's. For the Symbolists,
the city is sinister and otherworldly, but Akhmatova approaches
it with fondness and familiarity. The ugliness of modernity holds
a morbid attraction for the Symbolists; Akhmatova prefers to
see Petersburg's historical beauty. The rare instance of the pen-
etration of the modern city in her poetry occurs, oddly, in the single

poem which deals directly with the Petersburg of literary tradition ("Verses about Petersburg"): "The wind, suffocating and severe,/ Sweeps the soot from black chimneys . . ./Oh, the Emperor is displeased/With his new city" (Ch 209).

Much more typical of Akhmatova's preference for historical Petersburg is the image in the preceding stanza: "Once again is the cathedral of St. Isaac's/Arrayed in molten silver."

It is the old Petersburg, the familiar Petersburg, the Petersburg of history which captures the imagination of the poet, not the modernity of the contemporary metropolis which so intrigued, in different ways, the Symbolists and the Futurists. This fondness for the city of Peter and of Catherine, the city of Pushkin and Dostoevsky, is evident in Akhmatova's choice of images for her early work. In more recent compositions, the nostalgia for the city's great past becomes explicit:

> *The Russia of Dostoevsky . . .*
>
> *. . .*
>
> *The stern and straight Liteyny grows dark,*
> *Not yet disgraced by the modern,*
> *And vis-à-vis to me live—Nekrasov*
> *And Saltykov . . . To each a memorial*
> *Plaque. . . .*[5]

Akhmatova is extremely receptive to the Petersburg mystique, to the great literary tradition and the rich and colorful cultural history of the city. Unlike the Symbolists, however, she does not proceed from mystique to mystery. Her direction is opposite, toward the simplicity and clarity of concrete images. While the grandeur and magnificence—and the malevolence—are deeply sensed, Akhmatova's predominant attitude is a familiar one, even proprietary. It is "my" city; "our" city. At a later period, in a brief poem about Leningrad under bombardment, her sincere, possessive feeling for the entire city rises in a cry from the heart: "Trenches are dug in the garden,/No lights burn./Petersburg orphans/Children mine!/. . . .[6]

The great city on the Neva had been "blessed with her cradle"; it was home. Its streets and bridges and parks had been the background for her love, as they are the background for the love motif in her poetry.

It is in this connection that a comparison between Akhmatova's poems and the Symbolists' urban poetry may be made: love set against the background of the city, rather than the traditional nineteenth-century setting of love against nature. While the motives for the choice of such a background were quite different in each case, the results are often surprisingly similar. The cult of artificiality and the supposed hatred of nature which are proper to the Symbolists, and which in part led them to urban themes, are entirely foreign to Akhmatova. Her book *At the Edge of the Sea,* her impressions of the Bezhetsk area of Tver province and her feeling for the Russian countryside clearly demonstrate her difference from the Symbolists in this regard. Nevertheless, Akhmatova's love for Petersburg makes the urban theme quite as prominent in her work as it is in the poetry of the Symbolists.

Similarly, Akhmatova's interpretation of the love motif as deceit and betrayal produced a sequence of poems in which adultery, illicit relationships, and even licentiousness are central; the Symbolists' fascination for the depravities of the night city often led to parallel settings. The prostitutes and fallen women on the streets of Bryusov's Petersburg have at times a certain similarity with the deceived or deceiving heroines in Akhmatova's poems. Such a scene might well have occurred in one of Bryusov's or Blok's poems:

> *In the sky, the moon hangs scarcely alive*
> *Among the streaming, small clouds,*
> *And at the palace a gloomy guard*
> *Looks angrily at the hands of the tower clock.*
>
> *Homeward goes an unfaithful wife,*
> *Her face preoccupied and stern, . . .* (P 88)

In Akhmatova's poems, a woman on the street alone sometimes suggests an assignation. She noted in a critical article on Pushkin, that a woman "on the corner of a small square is the symbol of an adulteress."[7]

The night city fascinated Bryusov: "I praise the joys of the long street,/Where with daring glance and loathsome laughter/Prostitutes offer love. . . ."[8] For Bryusov, however, the city was the subject; for Akhmatova it is a setting.

Alexander Blok's poems taken from the life of the night city are in many instances parallel in setting to some of Akhmatova's early poems; both poets were, after all, part of the same milieu. Akhmatova's "Cabaret Artistique," for example, is very close in spirit to Blok's poems which deal with the Bohemian and artistic life of pre-Revolutionary Petersburg. The city for Blok was a "terrible world" inhabited by "small black people and drunken red dwarfs."[9]

In Akhmatova's poetry, the night city never overwhelms the dominant motif:

> *Yes, I loved them, those night gatherings,—*
> *On a small table, icy glasses,*
> *Over black coffee, that scented, delicate steam,*
> *The heavy, winter heat of the redhot stove,*
> *The acid humor of the literary joke*
> *And my lover's first glance, helpless and*
>   *frightful.* (BS 161)

The erotism which might be expected in varying degrees in Symbolist poetry of the night city is extremely restrained in Akhmatova's poetry. Most often, erotic undercurrents are suggested only obliquely by a glance, a touch, a gesture—as in the above example and in "Cabaret Artistique." Frankly erotic passages are in general few, and derive from the nature of the dominant motif rather than from any preoccupation with the decadence of the night city.

Indeed, while Akhmatova shares important characteristics with the Symbolists, any attempt at positive comparison results in more qualifications than there are similarities. The contrast was very aptly stated (although in a quite different context) by Zhirmunsky: "There [i.e., among the Symbolists] it is not a matter of the soul, but of the spirit."[10] Rather than intellectual or mystical conception of the city, Akhmatova's response to it is emotional in nature. Her feeling is *for* Petersburg, rather than *of* Petersburg.

Predictably, Tsarskoe Selo, the scene of Akhmatova's school years and early married life, is treated in the same fond and familiar way. The same proprietary feeling which made of the capital a personal possession encompasses the resplendent history of Tsarskoe Selo within a circle of highly personal associations. In dealing with the classical majesty of both Tsarskoe Selo and Petersburg, Akhma-

tova consciously avoids a grandiose style. Stately images alternate
with the most common ones; there is no comparison or attempt
at transition. The grand and the mundane mingle inseparably.

In later years, Tsarskoe Selo calls forth a nostalgia for a way of
life long past, for a love that once was; in one poem, Akhmatova
calls the town "my squandered inheritance" (I 15). The pointless
destruction of the lovely old town by the Germans in the Second
World War was a deep personal tragedy for the poet.

> *They burned my little toy town,*
> *And into the past I have no loophole left.*
> *There was a fountain there, green benches*
> *And in the distance the immensity of the*
>   *Czars' park.*
> *At Shrovetide—pancakes, bumpy roads and*
>   *sleighs,*
> *In April—the smell of mould and of earth,*
> *And the first kiss. . . . (6)*

The motif of Russia's cities combines here with national and
historical motifs, as well as the all-pervasive love motif. The touch-
ingly proprietary attitude of the first line suggests the irreverence
of familiarity which is so characteristically contrasted to the grandeur of Petersburg and the magnificence of the Summer Residence.
The rather ordinary and humble images—the traditional Shrovetide
pancakes, the bumpy roads, the little Finnish sleighs with their
multitude of bells—appear side by side with the splendor of the
Czars' Village suggested in the almost passing reference to the
immensity of the imperial park. In seven lines, Akhmatova evokes
both the Tsarskoe Selo of history and the home of her youth.
The last line lends not only a special significance to the series of
images, but a particular pathos to the moving statement in the
first two lines.[11]

The same love which Akhmatova feels for her "toy town" is
extended to other cities of her homeland: golden Bakhchisaray,
ancient Kherson and Voronezh of history are evoked for a moment
in all their cultural associations—to serve as background for what
appears to be extremely personal reminiscence. Bakhchisaray's
"pure fountains" recall Pushkin, and an eagle sweeping down from
its bronze gates suggests briefly the great days of imperial expansion.

The focus, however, narrows to a few dead leaves swirling on an unnamed stair where a final parting took place (BS 130). Kherson's domed cathedrals bring momentarily to mind the role of the city in Russia's history and in the history of Russian Orthodoxy,—in a poem of which the principal subject is love's pain (Ch 199). The slopes of Voronezh breathe the memory of Kulikovo Field, and the great Russian triumph merges subtly with the triumphant passion of the poetic person (I 32). Pavlovsk, Kislovodsk, Novgorod rise in Akhmatova's poetry, and in all but the shortest poems pass into a variation on the motif of love.[12]

Kiev, the Mother of Russian Cities, is the single subject of another poem; here, the love motif and personal reminiscence is replaced by a kind of national reminiscence (which is, incidentally, highly productive in her most recent work). The playful, surprise ending is typical for the irreverence of fond familiarity with which Akhmatova approaches the great cities of her homeland:

> *Wide open are swung the gates,*
> *The lindens are threadbare like beggars,*
> *And dark is the dry gilt*
> *Of the indestructible, concave wall.*
>
> *Filled with sounding are the altars and*
> *   crypts,*
> *And beyond the broad Dnepr, the ringing*
> *   flies.*
> *Thus does Mazeppa's heavy bell*
> *Boom over the square of St. Sophia.*
>
> *Ever more threatening it swells, inexorable,*
> *As though heretics were being executed here,*
> *And in the woods across the river, reconciled,*
> *It delights the fluffy little vixens.* (AD 55)

This is the impression which Akhmatova's cities produced on the critic Leonid Grossman:

These "stone beauties," to use Turgenev's words, not only serve as background for those love tales which are locked into the economical lines of Akhmatova's fragments; they are also material, in itself valuable, for her remarkable word-graphics.... Noteworthy is Anna Akhmatova's partiality to architectural masses, to that beauty of the world which was created

by hand, in which the deepest essence of the beautiful has been expressed. . . .
Whence in the poetry of Anna Akhmatova this abundance of cupolas,
towers, vaults, arches. Out of her elegies momentarily and monumentally
emerge the high vaults of churches, palaces . . . the white arches of the
Smolny cathedral. . . .

Not only in the quick impressions of the cities of Russia does
Akhmatova capture—often in one expressive and picturesque
epithet—the feeling of her country, but also by the briefest suggestion she can convey the limitless expanse of rural Russia. In
the poem above, the forests and broad plains beyond the Dnepr
flicker for a moment, remote and unchanging. The feather grass
of the Volga steppes, a dilapidated gate creaking in the wind of
the vast, indistinct spaces of Tver province, the bleak shores of
the northern sea—through such images does she suggest the immensity of her homeland. In all this expanse, there are "Mysterious, dark settlements,/Repositories of prayer and toil" (BS
146).

Grossman continues with his impressionistic reading of Akhmatova's poetry:

"And by some kind of miracle, through the momentary sketch
of a flickering image before us, there spread out immense, bound-
less and sad spaces, with their villages, gardens, pastures, parks,
rivers, seas. Out of the intimate circle of feminine lyrics, imper-
ceptibly but distinctly, in all its innumerable natural and cultural
contrasts, emerges Russia. . . ."[13]

CHAPTER 5

Themes of the Russian
Cultural Heritage

BY the phrase "innumerable natural and cultural contrasts," Grossman intended of course a great deal more than simply those between the present and past of Russia's great cities, or between the cities themselves and the remote countryside. Two lines already quoted "Mysterious, dark settlements,/Repositories of prayer and toil" (BS 146), call forth a complex series of associations with the Old Russian, patriarchal way of life which had echoes through the nineteenth century, and which exists in certain fundamental national attitudes even today. Such villages were the heart and life of the Russian past; unchanging through centuries and removed from outside influences, they fostered the development of a unique world-view. In these "mysterious, dark settlements," Eastern Orthodoxy was interpreted, reinterpreted, and finally fixed into national forms. The forced superposition in the eighteenth century of foreign culture upon this stabilized society was traumatic; it was followed by two centuries of political, intellectual, and social upheaval, and became a prime motive force in Russia's great literature of the nineteenth century. Conventions of the earlier period died hard, and in many cases still find reflection in contemporary Russian society.

Like many of the nineteenth-century authors, Akhmatova draws upon this earlier, richly colorful level of culture for much of her thematic material and imagery. The choice of her Tatar ancestor's name as pseudonym is in itself significant; a constant backward glance toward Russia's cultural and historical past is necessary to the interpretation of many poems.

I *Historical Motifs*

A number of critics, confusing Akhmatova's *persona* with the poet herself, have misread the function of the literary imagery drawn from Russia's cultural history, and often imply that there is something Medieval Muscovite about the poet's world-view. Chudovsky, for example, observes very properly that there is "something Old Russian, ancient" in Akhmatova's poetry, but goes on to observe that "she is the last and only poet of Orthodoxy... It doesn't matter if she mentions Paris, automobiles, and literary cafés—all this only more strongly distinguishes her Old Russian soul."[1]

The fact is, of course, that there are many *personae* in Akhmatova's poems, and only one of these is characterized by Old Russian imagery. Some seem almost identifiable with the poet herself, while others can be quite remote from the real person. It is true that an important and most interesting *persona* is the one in whom "there flows a drop of Novgorod blood, like a piece of ice in frothy wine" (BS 146), and whose attitudes are fixed in the patterns of a rich cultural inheritance. It is nevertheless also true that the *persona* may appear as a fashionable lady in a feathered hat riding through the Bois de Boulogne, as a literary figure from the Bohemian world of pre-Revolutionary Petersburg; or as a provincial girl daydreaming in a hammock. She may be haughty or humble, forgiving or malicious, austere or frivolous—and to attempt to reconcile the many poetic persons is both unnecessary and misleading.

A sentimental and homesick émigré, Yuly Eykhenwald, wrote in 1923: "[Akhmatova's] personal songs flow from the depths of her nationality, and in general, she is so Russian, so Great Russian, that she slakes our thirst for our homeland with the bright streams of her verse."[2]

Russian émigré critics may perhaps be permitted judgments of such an impressionistic nature. The foreign critic, however, must beware of such formulations. He courts the danger of coming under the spell of the "Russian soul," a Western fiction which derives largely from misreadings of nineteenth-century Russian literature and popular myths about the post-Revolutionary émigrés. Still, on the other hand, he must recognize that poetry does not arise in a vacuum, that it depends to a greater or lesser extent upon a long cultural heritage. It is on this heritage that Akhmatova draws for a significant part of her literary imagery, and for the characterization of one of her most fascinating *personae*.

Akhmatova's cultural and historical imagery, which strikes her fellow-countrymen as extraordinarily "Russian," is not restricted to immediately recognizable national themes: the so-called "patriotic" poems about Russia in war or Revolution, the urban poetry with its peculiar blend of historical grandeur and lyrical emotion, or the relatively few poems which portray provincial Russia. Nor is this imagery represented principally by the motifs and devices borrowed from Russian folk poetry; her folk settings are always highly stylized and indicate poetic sophistication rather than some uncomplicated spiritual kinship with the Russian folk singer. While these elements in Akhmatova's poetry lend a specifically Russian flavor to many poems, it is the attitudes and roles frequently given the *persona* which suggest most effectively the older, submerged level of Russian culture.

II *Religious Motifs*

Frequently, for example, the heroine who has been cast aside by her lover is given the role of a homeless wanderer. If, as we have seen, the love motif and the imagery of the house are inseparably intertwined, the symbol of homelessness is a potent one in Akhmatova's poetry. The pathos of the heroine's situation, however, does not depend merely on the image of the empty, abandoned, or lost house.

The conception of the wanderer often includes the suggestion of the destitute pilgrim who has renounced the world, an orphan without shelter, a woman who is ill, poverty-stricken or in beggary.[3] She is meekly resigned to her lot and humble before her misfortune.

The very frequency of this setting would perhaps suggest a poetry which is lachrymose, maudlin, or feeble. Yet it is of such poems that the critic N.V. Nedobrovo wrote:

These torments, complaints and finally such extreme resignation—isn't this weakness of heart simple sentimentality? Not at all: rather, [Akhmatova's] speech is firm and self-assured; the very calm in the acceptance of pain and weaknesses, and ultimately the very abundance of poetically transformed torments—all this . . . discloses a lyric spirit which rather is hard than too soft or tearful, and rather clearly dominating than oppressed.[4]

The image of the weeping woman in Akhmatova's poetry is not a simple device to create sympathy for the heroine; if this were the case, a kind of commiseration would be achieved at best—and at worst, embarrassment on the part of the reader. The homeless, destitute wanderer meekly resigned to her fate must be seen in terms of Old Russian attitudes if her reactions are to be understood.

In Old Russian society, a prime virtue was charity. Its innocently unsophisticated interpretation was pity for the unfortunate, and it was practiced simply, for the most part by some form of alms-giving. In the West, and particularly in Western Protestant tradition, this version of charity has long been suspect as pharisaical; "The Lord helps those who help themselves" seems more acceptable as a proverb than the vaguely disturbing Russian counterpart, "Poverty is no crime." Similarly, meek resignation to one's lot seems a somewhat questionable virtue, even to Calvinists. The old Orthodox, however, respected resignation in trial as strength, and made the Early Christian parallel between the sufferings of the afflicted, the lame, and the poor, and the suffering of Christ. The asceticism of the Orthodox holy men derives in large part from this idea; the simplest—and sometimes quite mad—hermits and anchorites were held in sincere esteem. Rejection of the world, its comforts and possessions, was a not infrequent phenomenon; it did not always lead to the monastery, but quite often to pilgrimage or a seemingly aimless wandering over the land. Renunciation of worldly things resulted typically from some great personal tragedy. These pilgrims were considered close to God, and their prophecies were carefully heeded.

Such figures appear directly in Akhmatova's poetry, not in any historical setting, but in contemporary life. We may recall the example of a poem quoted above, in which a wanderer prophesies in tones recalling Isaiah or Jeremiah, or the poem "To My Sister" (BS 144), in which the heroine, after misfortune, visits a monk in the forest. He admonishes her to forget "the home of her fathers" and to accept the life of poverty. She leaves him—*i divyasya i raduyas' mnogo*—"both marvelling and rejoicing greatly."

By using the convention of attitudes drawn from the Russian past, Akhmatova is permitted an extraordinary compression in her poetry. Within a single couplet, she can suggest love lost, consequent renunciation of the world, and the life of a pilgrim or anchorite: "And long since have my lips/Not kissed, but they prophesy" (BS 156).[5]

Interpretations depending upon such conventions can be difficult for non-Russian readers, particularly in extremely laconic poetry. Even in the great novels of the nineteenth century, Western readers often have difficulties in understanding motives derived from attitudes fixed in older periods of Russian culture. What appears to be weakness and self-immolation is, within the religious convention, strength and self-abnegation.

"The immemorial Russian temptation: self-abnegation, resignation, martyrdom, meekness, poverty—recalling Tyutchev, Tolstoy, and Dostoevsky, fascinates [Akhmatova] as well.[6]

Behind the image of the suffering, weeping woman, many of Akhmatova's critics have sensed the stern and severe figure of an Old Russian anchorite. "In general, wrote Chudovsky, "her Orthodoxy is Nestorian, not Byzantine, stifling and cloying, but Northern, sad, barren, akin to fens and scrub pine. . . ."[7]

The heroine's humble resignation and calm renunciation of the world strongly suggest a figure from an earlier Russia. In one poem, abandoned by her lover, she says to her victorious rival: "I shall not blame you . . ./Put on my clothes . . ./And I went away alone, yielding,/Yielding my place to another,/And I wandered uncertainly, like a blind woman/On an unfamiliar, narrow path" (Ch 208).

This pattern of love lost, meek acceptance, complete forgiveness, rejection of home and worldly possessions, and ultimately an aimless wandering forms the basis for many of Akhmatova's poems.[8]

> *Your white house and quiet garden*
> *I will leave,*
> *Let life be empty and radiant.*[9] (BS 95)

> *And now, less corporeal than the dead,*
> *In my inconsolable wandering. . . .*[10] (BS 166)

> *You don't love me at all,*
> *And you never will.*
> . . .
> *Why then every evening must I pray for you?*
> *Why then, having left my husband*
> *And my curly-headed child,*
> *Having left my beloved city*
> *And my own homeland,*
> *Do I wander, a black beggarwoman,*
> *About a foreign capital?* (P 78)

In this brief excerpt, the motif of love as pain and betrayal is again associated with homelessness. *Rodnaya storona* suggests a complex of national associations which the translation "home-land" cannot convey; the epithet *kudryavy* ("curly-haired") has a certain flavor of Russian folk poetry about it. But what is really national in this poem is the traditionally Russian image of a desti-tute beggarwoman wandering in some foreign place.

Georgy Ivanov included in his reminiscences *Peterburgskie zimy* an anecdote concerning Akhmatova which captures the quality of the poems of this type. The story came, according to Ivanov, from the rumors circulated about Akhmatova in Parisian émigré circles during the first years of exile. Although the material is presented as true, Ivanov's book is highly impressionistic,[11] and it may never have occurred at all. The essence of this story is common enough in the folklore of many peoples. Nevertheless, knowing Akhmatova's vagaries in dress, it could have happened:

> Do you know, Anya was once walking along the Mokhovaya. With a bag. She was carrying some flour, it seems. She tired, and stopped to breathe. It was winter; she was poorly dressed. Some woman walked past . . . gave her a kopeck. *Vozmite, Khrista radi* . . . Anna hid that kopeck behind the icon. . . . She was saving it. . . .[12]

This anecdote could well be the setting of an Akhmatova poem; certainly it has the elements of one: the city street, the cold, the weariness, the poor dress, the empty religiosity of the formula *Khrista radi* coupled with the deeply religious overtones of the gesture of almsgiving, the kopeck as a portent, the religious-super-stitious act of concealing the coin behind an icon. All this might have come from a poem in *The Plantain* or *Anno Domini*.

Poverty is an important aspect in the complex of humility, renunciation of the world, and homeless wandering. As in Ivanov's anecdote, the minor motif of dress merges with this complex in the suggestion of poverty. The heroine may appear "In this grey workday dress/On run-down heels . . ." (Ch 203). In a striking juxtaposition of these motifs, even the Muse is conceived in this manner: "And the Muse in a ragged kerchief/Sings lingeringly and despairingly" (BS 134).

Humility and self-abnegation combine in a poverty which is somehow triumphant: "For you I gave up my birthright,/And in exchange I ask nothing./Whence even the rags of an orphan/I wear like wedding garments" (AD 47).

And with the poverty, affliction and infirmity: "But claw, claw in rage/At my consumptive breast,/So that the blood rush from my throat/More quickly onto the bed. . . ." (P 85).

In a poem mentioned briefly above, where the heroine makes a pilgrimage to a hermit living in a hut deep in a pine forest, the hermit prophesies: "Ailing, you will sleep on straw/And have a blessed end" (BS 144).

The suggestion here, of course, is that the hermit is calling the heroine to the life of devotion. Indeed, the suggestion of a nun is inescapable among all these images of self-denial, renunciation of the world, triumphant suffering and poverty, humility, and meek resignation. What is remarkable is that Akhmatova keeps the suggestion a suggestion; the heroine is never cast in the role of a nun. A comparison may be inferred, but never made directly:

> *There was no temptation. Temptation lives*
> *in quiet,*
> *It wearies him who fasts, oppresses the*
> *saintly . . .*
> *And in the May midnight over the young*
> *nun*
> *It cries, wearily, like a wounded eagle . . .*
> *But these licentious, these amiable sinners*
> *Have never known the embrace of iron arms.* (AD 61)

In only three instances is the word "nun" used, and of these, one is a disclaimer—probably prompted by the excesses of the critics, who were fond of identifying not only the poetic person, but Akhmatova herself, as a "moral nun": "Not a shepherdess nor a queen,/Nor yet a nun am I" (Ch 203).

The following selection is characteristic of the figurative indirection she employs in suggesting the nun. The pattern here, while not entirely obvious at first glance, repeats that of a number of poems discussed above: renunciation of the world after great personal tragedy, wandering lost in difficult circumstances, and finally quiet resignation.

> *I know, I know—once again skis*
> *Will begin scraping dryly;*

> In the blue sky a russet moon,
> The meadow is so delightfully sloping.
>
> In the palace, little windows shine,
> Made distant by the silence;
> There is neither path nor road,
> Only the dark ice-holes.
>
> Willow, tree of the water-nymphs,
> Don't hinder me on my way;
> In your snowy branches the black daws,
> Give the black daws refuge. (Ch 212)

The first two lines of this poem, taken by themselves, seem to have little meaning beyond the obvious logic of the passage. It is typical, however, of Akhmatova's method of expressing rather complex abstracts by simple, concrete imagery: "to live," for example, is rendered in another poem "to go for walks, to kiss, and to grow old." In the context of the whole poem, the first two lines suggest that life will go on, that there is a tomorrow. The conversational style of the opening is typical; it is as though the heroine is in conversation with herself, or as though fragments of an earlier conversation keep running through her mind as it distractedly registers impressions of the world about her. She knows that others will ski again, that others will go on living in a world which she is forsaking. As she wanders through the snowy night, her homelessness and solitude are emphasized by the use of the familiar diminutive, *okoshki,* for the palace windows which shine warm and bright across the silent distance. This diminutive is not at all extraordinary in cultured speech; the intimate, conversational opening of the poem has prepared for it. By its very familiarity and informality, however, it introduces smoothly a cliché which has the flavor of folk speech—and which directly succeeds a quite sophisticated image on the standard literary level of the language. If the phrase *ni tropinki, ni dorozhki,* may occur in the conversation of cultured Russians, it nevertheless carries a definitely Russian folk connotation; it adequately prepares for the abrupt shift in frame of reference to the folk level in the last stanza.

The dark ice-holes suggest death, and perhaps the momentary contemplation of suicide. Dark water more than once in Akhmatova's poetry symbolizes suicide or death (for example, "Do not drive me there/Where under the suffocating vault of the bridge/ The dirty water grows cold" [suicide], or "There, where there is a swan and dead water" [death]). While it may or may not have been intended here, there is a close parallel with the symbol of water/ river as it is used in the feminine genre of Russian folk lyrics. In the folk tradition, cold or rolling water/river symbolizes sadness, desertion or abandonment by the lover, loneliness. Veselovsky lists it among the major symbols of folk poetry.[13] In the last stanza, not only is the reference to the *rusalka,* or water-nymph, drawn directly from the Russian folk tradition, but the singularly significant image of the black daw is used in the folk sense, where it symbolizes a nun—and interestingly, at other times—a young girl in love. *("Sokol slovil galku/Molodets poymal devitsu;"* "The falcon caught the jackdaw/The young man caught the girl.")[14] Most often, however, the daw is a *chernichka-galochka,* a nun. Nikolay Klyuev, a folk poet and perhaps a folk mannerist, who was a contemporary and friend of Akhmatova in the days before the Revolution, used the symbol in this way: *"Galka-staroverka khodit v chyornoy ryaske"* (The jackdaw-Old Believer [woman] wears a black cassock).[15]

The symbol of the nun provides a key to the interpretation of the entire poem, which in its verbal compactness is a kind of riddle. Given the pattern established in so many other poems, it becomes clear that the speaker in the first lines has forsaken her home, presumably the palace in the distance, to wander in the dark winter night. The renunciation of the home, in the tradition, often follows great personal loss, which in Akhmatova's poetry can only be the loss of love. The heroine contemplates suicide briefly on her way—on her way, apparently, to the convent. As it so often happens in Akhmatova's poems, religious motifs are mixed with superstition and submerged relics of paganism. The heroine asks the willow, the pagan tree, the tree of the water nymphs, to give refuge to the black daws with whom she can now identify herself, just as she herself will be given refuge in the convent.

There are many interesting oppositions in this poem: in color (the *blanc-et-noir* technique is characteristic of Akhmatova), in levels of speech, but perhaps the most characteristic opposition is between the *rusalka* and the *galka,* between pagan, profane love and the religious life. In this opposition are represented the two spheres which contribute most to the Old Russian timbre of Akhmatova's lyrics: the religious and the folk motifs.

"Religion and poetry are two sides of one and the same coin," wrote Gumilyov. "Both require of man spiritual labor—but not in the name of a practical goal, like ethics or esthetics, but in the name of something higher, unknown. The leadership and rebirth of man belongs both to religion and poetry."[16]

Gumilyov was never quite able to relinquish the Romantic, and later specifically Symbolist, concept of the poet as seer or priest. His personal religion was of an ambiguous nature,[17] and was not significant in his early years. While he questioned the mystical and revelatory aspect of Symbolist poetry, he adopts in his own poetry a role similar to that of the Symbolist poet-priest. His rather muddy thinking on the relationship between religion and poetry is illustrated in the quotation above.

In Akhmatova's poetry, the religious content differs greatly from Gumilyov's, such as it is, and from that of the Symbolists. While Gumilyov's religious imagery and motifs often bear a striking resemblance to Akhmatova's,[18] the fundamental attitudes of the two poets could not have been more disparate.

To recall once again Zhirmunsky's comparison of Akhmatova with the Symbolists, this time in its original context, "There [among the Symbolists], it is a matter of the spirit, and not the soul." The poems in which religious imagery is prominent indicate, according to Zhirmunsky, "not mystical insight, but a firm and simple belief, which has become the basis of life: this old-fashioned, calm, and positive faith enters into life itself, acquires a complex historical and cultural existence, in ceremony, in habitual religious actions and in the outward signs of religious service."[19]

Zhirmunsky tends to accept the religious content of Akhmatova's poetry as springing from a genuine and deep personal faith. Whether this is the case, or whether the religious content represents merely a poetic device among others, is not important here. It is clear that Akhmatova intended this simple faith and Old Russian attitudes to be a fundamental trait of one of her most interesting *personae*.

It is the religious aspect of Akhmatova's poetry which has, since the early 1920's, most often come under critical fire. Lelevich attacked it sarcastically in part of an essay entitled "Blagochestivaya deva Anna" ("The Pious Maiden Anna"),[20] both recognizing and satirizing the Old Russian elements in the heroine's character. Trotsky, in *Literature and Revolution,* wrote:

> With perplexity do you read our anthologies of verse, especially those of the women—here is where indeed *bez boga ni do poroga* ("without God you cannot reach the doorstep"). The lyric circle of Akhmatova, Tsvetaeva, Radlova and other real and approximate poetesses, is very small. It includes the poetess herself, an unknown man in a bowler or with spurs, and without fail, God—minus any special distinguishing features. He is a trained, very comfortable and portable third person, quite housebroken, a friend of the home fulfilling from time to time the duties of doctor to feminine complaints. How this personage, who is no longer young, who is burdened with the personal and frequently troublesome demands of Akhmatova, Tsvetaeva and others, manages still in his free time to direct the fate of the universe, is simply inaccessible to the mind.[21]

If literary criticism lacked example for striking diversity of opinion on a single subject, the peculiar religiosity in Akhmatova's poems would provide an excellent one. It has been variously lauded and condemned on moral grounds, ignored or studied closely in critical essays, excoriated or defended from the most unusual critical vantage points—and in almost every case, has tempted the critic to witticism.

One of the most just critical formulae (and subsequently the most unjustly interpreted) was Boris Eykhenbaum's characterization of Akhmatova's poetic figure as *ne to monakhinya, ne to bludnitsa,* "half-nun, half-harlot." Taken from its context, it became a critical catch-phrase, distorted by adverse criticism into the suggestion of something distasteful, immoral and "of pernicious effect on the youth of the land."[22]

The original intent of Eykhenbaum's phrase, of course, was to characterize one of Akhmatova's most obviously striking juxtapositions in motifs: the juxtaposition of the religious themes with her dominant motif of passionate, earthly love. Although clearly not intended by Eykhenbaum, the phrase also suggests the markedly feminine quality of Akhmatova's poetry, her critics and reviewers never fail to mention this quality which is so easily sensed but so difficult to define. *Ne to monakhinya, ne to bludnitsa* is perhaps as accurate a description of a real woman as any other. Blok expressed the idea by calling Akhmatova a "Christian gypsy."

An impressionist critic wrote that "Anna is a moral nun, with a cross on her breast. . . . But this Christian is in love, and love is pagan. . . ."[23] Mark Slonim echoed such impressions: "Her volumes seemed chapters of a lyrical diary devoted to love, song and prayer; they sounded like the confession of a passionate nun who had fled the convent and opened her heart to earthly love, yet still wore a hair shirt."[24] Even Chudovsky, who among Akhmatova's critics came the closest to relating her religious motifs to her complex cultural inheritance, began his review of one of Akhmatova's volumes in this way:

Reading Akhmatova's *The White Flock,* the second book of her poems [*Evening* and *Rosary* had earlier appeared in a single volume], I thought: "Hasn't Akhmatova yet had her hair shorn to enter a nunnery?" . . . I should not be surprised if her next volume turned out to be a prayer book.[25]

Certainly, there is within Akhmatova's poetry sufficient material to justify such critical flights. Her very vocabulary is rich in Biblical and liturgical words: chasubles, icons, King David, angels and archangels, incense, St. Eudoxia, crucifix. As Chudovsky noted, there seems to be no substantive which cannot be modified by the word "God's": God's sunlight, God's garden, God's birds, even God's lilacs. If it rains, "God is not merciful to reapers and gardeners." If it is too hot, "The sun has become God's wrath." If it is cold, "The first ray is the gift of God." Winter is "whiter than the vaults of the Smolny Cathedral."

Even in frankly religious verse, such an abundance of Biblical and liturgical images might seem extreme. As Chudovsky observed, however, "With every other poet, these metaphors would seem mannered pretention, but with Akhmatova, they so harmonize with her whole monastic appearance that they emerge living and sincere."[26]

Intrigued by the effect of the juxtaposition of sacred and profane love, many poets—especially women—attempted to imitate it. Generally they failed; the outcome was something like the poem written by Liza in Nabokov's novel *Pnin*. Nabokov notes that in the 1920's the émigrés grouped around the Rotonde in Paris attempted to write poems in the manner of Akhmatova. Here is Liza's:

> *I have put on a dark dress*
> *And am more modest than a nun.*
> *A crucifix of ivory*
> *Is above my cold bed.*

> *But the fires of fabulous orgies*
> *Burn through my oblivion,*
> *And I whisper the name George—*
> *Your golden name!*[27]

The epigones failed to reproduce, among other things, Akhmatova's characteristic restraint. The juxtaposition of the sacred and the profane in the following lines is of purely literary origin, a parallel to juxtaposition in Lermontov's *Demon:* "But I swear to you by the angels' garden,/By the miracle-working icon do I swear,/And the nights of our smouldering passion . . ." (AD 50).

There are few examples of such direct juxtapositions. Even in poems without religious imagery, desire is treated with restraint: "Again he touched my knee/With an almost untrembling hand" (Ch 175).

Passion itself is suggested in an oddly indirect way, through Akhmatova's use of the impersonal expression: "But again it is night. And again/In moist languor to kiss his shoulders" (AD 48).

Such passages as these are rare, however, and any characterization of Akhmatova's poetry as "erotic" is gross and misleading. The complete absence of the passionate embrace is notable; in most cases, the erotic aspect of love must be adduced from hints of the most oblique nature.

Critics generally ignored this restraint in their descriptions of the "passionate nun."

Oddly, one of the best statements concerning Akhmatova's religious motifs came from the 1926 edition of the *Bolshaya sovetskaya entsiklopediya.* The critical intention of the statement was clearly negative, but with a little qualification, and taken from context, it is more correct than perhaps its authors intended: "Religious motifs—icons, prayers, churches, vows, sinfulness and so on—are not deep. . . . They are rather an esthetic form of the archaic way of life of the gentry, rather than real religion."

When unmistakably religious imagery is employed, and even when Akhmatova makes use of Old Russian images of martyrdom, humility, poverty, pilgrimage, and so forth, it is obvious that the poet is expressing something quite different from religious sentiment.

> Under the roof of my chill, empty dwelling
> I do not count the deadening days,
> I read the Epistles,
> The words of the psalmist.
> But the stars shine blue, but the frost
>   is feathery,
> And every meeting is more marvellous,—
> And in the Bible, a red maple leaf
> Marks the Song of Songs. (BS 113)

Quickly setting a mood of loneliness through the characteristic symbol of the empty house, Akhmatova conjures up for a moment the vision of a woman at her devotional reading on a cold winter's day. The stern severity of St. Paul's Epistles and the impassioned pleas of the psalmist suggest both the humble resignation and yet the longing of the heroine during the days when her beloved is absent. The mood changes with the expectation of another meeting, and the joy of reunion is paralleled in the exultation of the *Song of Songs*. Here, among the pages of the *Song of Songs* is pressed a red maple leaf, in memory of another, earlier meeting in the fall.

Although the poem is built on religious images, there is nothing of a truly religious nature in it; it is rather a statement of earthly love, of longing and of anticipated reunion. Compare the following excerpt: " . . . Three years ago, Palm Sunday. . . . My hand, on which the wax had dropped [from a procession candle]/Trembled, receiving a kiss,/And my blood sang: ye blessed one,/rejoice!" (P 87).

This poem is filled with liturgical images: Palm Sunday, a prayerful *(bogomolny)* evening, when people walked in procession with candles fluttering in the black wind, the church bells ringing comfort. Here again, the subject of the poem is hardly the Triumphal Entry; the love theme is richly expressed in liturgical imagery, and the exultation of the ceremony repeats, or is fused with, the exultation of love.

Here, as in the preceding example, the love motif is expressed almost entirely in terms of religious imagery; more typically, the pervasive religious motif is only incidental in the treatment of the major motif. It occurs in unconscious gestures once religious in nature but which have long since lost their original force; in appeals to the Almighty which have now become mild interjections.

"I have learned to live simply, wisely,/To look at the sky and pray to God" (Ch 197) scarcely indicates the choice of the life of devotion; the second line is merely another way of saying "to live simply, wisely." "I pressed with both hands/The chain of the cross on my breast" (BS 126) represents, in a love lyric, no sudden surge of religious scruples, but the habitual action of a woman startled. "I set him free/On Annunciation Day" (BS 149) has no especial religious significance; it suggests rather the old-fashioned practice of dating by church holiday. (The folk tone of the following line, "And the grey dove returned," complements the suggestion.) Compare: Eastertide, Palm Sunday, the Feast of St. Agrafena, and "white, white All-Saints day."

The majority of religious references are of this type; they suggest a Russian society of earlier days, permeated with Orthodox expressions and symbols. We have here the product of highly ritualized religion, and there is in this respect a striking resemblance to the attitudes and expressions of Italian and Spanish women. It is interesting to note that in the poems where there is no clearly definable attempt to evoke Old Russian associations, the habitual gestures of religious origin frequently occur, and the Holy Name itself seems at times little more than a conversational filler.

Sometimes, however, there is a reflection of a deeper level of Orthodox associations: "The wept-out autumn, like a widow/In black clothes, darkens every heart./ . . ./And so it will be, until the quietest snow/Takes pity on the woeful and weary one . . ." (AD 60).

The simile of the widow does not necessarily suggest any specifically Old Russian or Orthodox associations, although, to be sure, the widow figures among the orphaned, the halt, the crazed, and the homeless wanderers who were the objects of both respect and charity in Old Russian society. Rather, it is the epithet *tishayshiy* which has specifically Orthodox overtones. *Tishayshiy,* in its first meaning, is simply "most quiet," but its use by the Orthodox have given it the meaning of most meek, most mild. It is in this context that the czar, as head of the Russian church, is given among his other titles the rather anomalous title *tishayshiy*. In the above poem, the epithet is connected directly with pity for the weary and heavy-laden.

III *Superstition*

The Old Russian flavor of the religiosity Akhmatova employs in her imagery is complemented by the frequent evocation of ancient folk supersititions, which along with Orthodoxy were part and parcel of the Old Russian culture. In many poems, there is the suggestion of the folk *dvoeverie* ("double belief," that is, in both religion and superstition). The poetic person professes belief in signs and portents, she asks the cuckoo to tell her future, and turns to witches for a potion: "Or that I shall beg of the healingwomen/ A small root in spell-casting water" (AD 50).

The "double belief" at its most elemental level is suggested in the following stanza—highly stylized, as always: "I took with me only the cross/You gave me the day of your betrayal,—/So that the wormwood steppe should bloom,/And the winds should sing like the sirens" (BS 127).

The poetic person may "tell the future" at Epiphany (that is, *gadat'*, is to tell the future from wax or lead dropped into cold water as part of a rather involved folk ritual, V 230; compare V 247); she may "cast spells" (*koldovat'* BS 123); and "prophesy" (*prorochit'* BS 156). Her house can be filled with the rustling of lindens and the *pereklichki domovykh* ("the calls of the household sprites," something on the order of Slavic penates, I 13). From time to time, a ghost flickers momentarily on the "worn red plush of the armchairs"; smoke that hangs low is a sign of imminent misfortune, but "I am not afraid . . . I carry a dark blue silk thread for luck" (Ch 198).

The heroine wears a magic ring, given by her lover to protect her from love (P 74); shades from the past appear in her rooms (AD 45, BS 158); the eyes of mysterious, ancient faces follow her (Ch 174), and she believes in "curses from crumbling old books" (Ch 202). Second sight, as has been noted above, is suggested more than once; the poetic person has "secret presentiments" (AD 61).

For the most part, like the superficial elements of religiosity, superstition is part of the cultural pattern which colors Akhmatova's verse. At times, however, an awareness of supernatural phenomena seems to spring from a deeper level. When the poet adopts the role of prophetess, the quality of real superstitious belief is felt. In the poem "Beyond the Lake the Moon Stood Still," not a single word suggesting the supernatural (of which, it is true, Akhmatova is fond) is used. But a chill awareness of the dark powers suffuses the poem, which would seem to have been inspired only by a deep emotional experience.

> *Beyond the lake the moon stood still,*
> *And it seems a window opened*
> *Into a suddenly silent, brightly lighted*
> *   house*
> *Where something bad has happened.*
>
> *Was it that the owner was brought home dead,*
> *Or that his wife ran away with her lover,*
> *Or that a little girl disappeared*
> *And her slipper found near the mill?*
>
> *You can't tell from the earth. Sensing*
> *A terrible misfortune, we at once fell*
> *   silent.*
> *The horned owls called mournfully,*
> *And the stifling wind howled in the*
> *   garden.* (AD 45)

In another setting, again a supernatural awareness is treated— this time in a lighter mood, arch and charming. This later work (1940) plays with an idea which had been often suggested in Akhmatova's earlier poetry: "I myself am not of those/Who are subject to others' spells./I myself . . . but then, I don't/Give away my secrets for nothing" (from "Khozyayka").

In a poem from *Anno Domini,* the suggestion of a witch is also used; here, superstition and religion are directly juxtaposed: "They used to banish such women to convents,/And to burn them on high pyres" (AD 46).

It is possible, of course, to read both lines within an entirely religious context, particularly since the role of martyr is so frequently employed. Nevertheless, the examples above could justify the second interpretation—and perhaps in Akhmatova's extremely compressed style, both were intended.

IV *The Folk Tradition*

If Akhmatova draws on peasant traditions for many images, it is not surprising that she should also draw on the lyric genre of Russian folk songs. In Russian folk tradition, the lyric song is exclusively the women's genre. Its subject matter is very close to Akhmatova's own: the cruel husband, the unfaithful lover, the abandoned girl or wife. While this subject matter is scarcely confined to Russian folk poetry, its forms of expression have long since crystallized into distinctly national ones.

Directly in the tradition of *zhenskaya dolya* (woman's sad lot), Akhmatova wrote: "For you I accepted a sad lot,/A tormenting lot . . ."[28] (V 241).

Such obvious borrowings from the folk tradition are confined largely to the three earliest collections; there, they account for some of Akhmatova's most well-known and justly famous poems. Folk settings *per se* seem to be less frequently used after *The White Flock,* although echoes of the tradition and folk themes of a submerged type remain characteristic. It is significant that in 1962, Akhmatova published two *pesenki,* folk songs, in the peasant style.

During Akhmatova's earliest period, folk poets such as Esenin were the rage in literary Petersburg; the erstwhile Acmeist Sergey Gorodetsky recognized the talent of the outstanding folk poet Nikolay Klyuev, and sponsored him in literary salons. Gorodetsky's own "folk" creations were little more successful than those of the other folk mannerists of the day.

Akhmatova, however, was not a folk mannerist; that is to say, she did not attempt to create "folk poetry." She borrowed a few fixed forms from the tradition, a number of settings, images, symbols, but ignored the rigidly fixed rules of the genre. In most cases, the sophisticated, experimental poet can be seen through the colorful but inevitable pattern of the folk lyric. Her *Pesenka* is typical; the folk flavor of the song is inescapable, yet scarcely any of the rules of composition for such songs are followed—notably the syntactical parallelisms, in which a line or couplet is drawn from nature and the succeeding one describes the heroine; more importantly, the highly personal ending is entirely atypical of the folk genre.

> *At sunrise,*
> *I sing of love,*
> *On my knees in the garden*
> *I'm pulling pigweed.*
>
> *I tear it out and throw it away—*
> *May it forgive me.*

> *I see that a barefoot girl*
> *Is weeping at the wattle fence.*

> *I am frightened by the ringing wails*
> *Of woe's voice;*
> *Stronger and stronger is the warm smell*
> *Of the dead pigweed.*

> *A stone instead of bread*
> *Will be my reward.*
> *Above me is only the sky,*
> *And with me your voice.* (V 242)

The often-quoted *"luchshe b mne chastushki zadorno vyklikat' "* ("Better for me to sing out chastushki" [a simple folk form, usually quatrains] BS 168) holds more closely to the original pattern, but the final couplet contains a mention of God which is not acceptable in the areligious genre. The *Skazka o chyornom koltse,* "[Folk] Tale of the Black Ring," is done in the manner of the Pushkin *skazki,* although it is merely another setting for the love motif. Akhmatova's longest work, *At the Edge of the Sea (U samogo morya),* alternates devices taken directly from the *skazka* tradition with religious motifs and highly subjective emotions which are entirely inadmissable within the convention. More suitable to the religious motifs are the *dukhovnye stikhi,* which Akhmatova modifies in her compositions in *Zhitiya (Lives).*

It is sufficient to cite only one poem in which Akhmatova uses a folk setting as her dominant theme to demonstrate the effectiveness of her method:

> *Since the Feast of St. Agrafena*[29]
> *He has kept my raspberry-colored kerchief.*
> *He is silent, and exults, like King David.*
> *In his frosty cell the walls are white,*
> *And no one talks with him.*

> *I shall go, and stand on the threshold,*
> *I shall say: "Give me back my kerchief."* (Ch 204)

The dating by the church calendar in the first line sets the Old Russian tone for the poem, and the folk symbol in the second reinforces it. In women's folk lyrics, the kerchief may replace the ribbon as a symbol for maidenhood. (The raspberry, also; the raspberry-colored kerchief compounds the symbol.) More often, the hair-ribbon is used—compare, in the poem using the *chastushka* form, "to loose the ribbon from my tight braid." Even in a poem which has no relation to folk tradition, the symbol is used: "I shall send you an awesome present/My secret, soft kerchief" (AD 50).

The lover, as has been noted, is often cast as an indifferent, distant person after the act of love. His distance is expressed through the image of King David, and his coldness suggested by the cold, white walls of his cell: he is sufficient unto himself. In the final couplet, the symbolism of the house is suggested once more; the heroine cannot enter his dwelling, but can only call from the threshold.

The dominant motif of love's pain occurs here once again in the *tema* of rejection and abandonment. Akhmatova's subject and her approach to it are scarcely new or original; both, indeed, are characteristic for the feminine folk lyric. Yury Tynyanov, an able and sensitive critic, felt that Akhmatova's admirable technical abilities were stifled by the unique subject, that "she is a prisoner of her own theme. The theme directs her, dictates her images, subtly permeates her whole poetry."[30] As an epigraph to his article, he chose the line from "Lot's Wife,"—*I bystrye nogi k zemle prirosli* ("And her swift feet were rooted to the ground"). "But it is curious," Tynyanov continued, "that when Akhmatova began, she was new and valuable not because of her themes, but in spite of them." It is not so very curious when one considers that what appears to be a narrow and single-minded preoccupation is actually a conscious self-limitation to "love . . . which is tormenting, morbidly perceptive and despairing." It is this single theme which gives such an extraordinary unity to each of Akhmatova's volumes, and indeed, to the whole series of works published between 1912 and 1922. To Eykhenbaum, Akhmatova's poetry seemed "something like a long novel."[31] The success of Akhmatova's extreme verbal economy depends in large part on the conventions she has gradually established in the "long novel"; many poems would be impossible to interpret fully without them. The unique motif, and the single point of view toward it, provide integration for countless disconnected secondary motifs, which may range widely from details of dress and interiors, through Russia's great cities, and endless open plains, through the history and culture of a people.

Of the thematic wealth in the brief lyric poems of Akhmatova, Leonid Grossman wrote:

These extremely laconic lyrics are filled with such an abundance of emotions, images, memories and thoughts, that in the short strophes, the slim volumes, is concentrated one of the greatest lyrical riches of the present day. The work of Akhmatova, which has often been considered too restricted, too narrow in motifs, with a partiality for the one dominant of "undivided love," has in fact a wide variation of lyric themes and poetic devices. Along with the external compression, the range of her creation is so wide and deep, the tight forms of her little poems are so filled with drama, each image opens such unlimited possibility of new visions and conceptions, that we understand the admission of the poet:

> *Ten years of a sinking heart and*
> *of cries,*
> *And all my sleepless nights*
> *I put into a quiet word. . . .*[32]

CHAPTER 6

Vocabulary

THE poets of the post-Symbolist generation are characterized in large part by their attitudes toward the word in poetry. These attitudes may in turn be defined in terms of a reaction against Symbolism which resulted, in various quarters, in quite different approaches. Some of these were discussed in the chapter on Acmeism. There was, however, a common feature in all the variety of approaches: the conception of the word in its original, primary denotation, as opposed to Symbolist connotation and acoustical suggestion.

The nature of the Acmeist reaction was toward a lexicon heavily weighted with words denoting concrete things, words bearing the suggestion of mass, weight, and texture.[1] The early Acmeists consciously strove toward restoring "thingness" to the word.

To some critics, the Acmeist tendency toward concreteness has seemed exaggerated; Gumilyov and Mandelstam have been reproached with coldness, objectivity. Blok found something foreign and cold in Gumilyov's poetry.[2] Lvov-Rogachevsky felt that in the effort to recreate brilliant gems (cf. Gumilyov's *Pearls*) or almost palpable stones (cf. Mandelstam's *Stone*), the poets reproduced only these inanimate objects, without creating any feeling for them. "Even the very Notre Dame de Paris, beautiful and triumphant, with Gothic arches reaching to the blue sky, they [the Acmeists] took apart into stones; they did not see the forest for the trees."[3] If Lvov-Rogachevsky's judgment seems narrow and harsh with regard to Gumilyov and Mandelstam, neither he nor any other critic has accused Akhmatova of coldness resulting from the Acmeist orientation to the material things of this world. Yet in Akhmatova's poetry, the deepest lyrical emotion is typically conveyed through words which signify the simplest, most ordinarily material things: a lintel, a glove, a stone, a hat plume.

Mochulsky described Akhmatova's reaction to the things about her in this manner:

Her work is characterized by plasticity in the physical and artistic sense; hers is a world of concrete forms, lines, mass and perspective. Each phenomenon in the external world calls forth in her a physio-psychological reaction; impressions are localized in space and time. . . . As a plastic artist, she feels the individuality and characteristic tone of the material.[4]

It is difficult to find a name for Mochulsky's "external phenomenon" which calls forth the "physio-psychological reaction." Eliot's famous "objective correlative" may be relevant here (both Eliot and Pound were influenced by Gautier, and at about the same time as Gumilyov and the Acmeists were). In any case, in Akhmatova's poetry, the "external phenomenon" is both itself and the reaction to it. The "external phenomenon" is not a symbol for the reaction; it remains its concrete, historical self, a "thing."[5] However one may choose to characterize Akhmatova's "things"—whether in terms of Mandelstam's formulation, or Mochulsky's "physio-psychological reaction," or the objective correlative—no explanation is so clear as the impression received from the reading of one of Akhmatova's poems. The following selection, for example, illustrates perhaps as well as any other the reaction against Symbolist abstractions and the return to the things of this earth:

> *Of flowers and inanimate things*
> *Pleasant is the smell in this house.*
> *Near their beds, heaps of vegetables*
> *Lie motley on the black earth.*
>
> *There are still wafts of cold air,*
> *But the mats have been taken from*
> *   the hotbeds.*
> *There's a pond there, such a pond*
> *Where the pond scum looks like brocade.*
>
> *And a small boy told me, scared,*
> *Quite excitedly and softly,*
> *That a big carp lives there,*
> *And with him, a big lady carp.* (Ch 190)

The subject of the poem is a small boy's wonder at discovering the world for himself. There is a series of concrete and quite humble images, ending with a pond. At mid-point in the poem, the imagery passes smoothly from ordinary to extraordinary; the "pond scum looks like brocade." The mood of wonderment in the last quatrain is thus prepared for; the boy's humorous assumption that one of the fish is a "lady," and his childish neologism *karasikha,* serve to communicate the freshness and innocence of his view.

When Akhmatova wrote in one of her poems, *"Zamechayu vsyo kak novoe"* ("I notice everything anew"), she was not just parroting Acmeist theory. Her poems often bring into focus words signifying quite ordinary objects or phenomena which might be ignored in other contexts. The pale, yellowish light which sometimes occurs on a winter's day, for example, is conjured up through a series of concrete images; even the flowers used in a simile to evoke the peculiar light are given a kind of reality, a physical existence in the experience of the poetic person:

> *When I went out, I was blinded*
> *By the transparent reflection on*
>   *things and faces,*
> *As though everywhere were lying petals*
> *Of those yellow-pinkish small roses,*
> *The name of which I have forgotten.* (AD 64)

This excerpt is taken from the second part of a rather long poem, and it concerns the reminiscence of a walk on a winter's day through the streets on Vassilevsky Island. The poem ends: "And on the bridge, through rusty hand-rails/Thrusting their mittened hands,/Children fed the speckled, greedy ducks/That bobbed in an inky icehole."

It is in the fresh perception of such ordinary and often humble things that Akhmatova's difference from the Symbolists, her "Acmeism," is most marked. For her, the "freshness of the word" was the *summum bonum:*

> *Isn't it the same for us to lose the*
>   *freshness of words*
> *And simplicity of feeling as for a*
>   *painter his vision,*
> *Or an actor his voice and movement*
> *And a beautiful woman her beauty?* (BS 109)

While the renewed perception of external phenomena and the "things of this world" are characteristic for Akhmatova, almost all her critics have overstated their case in this regard. What is a distinctive feature in Akhmatova's poetry—especially when comparing her to the Symbolists—need not necessarily occur in every poem. The preceding selection, for example, comes from a poem which is an entirely abstract statement, without concrete imagery, or renewed perception of concrete objects. Indeed, in her predominantly sad poetry, the distinctly positive attitude associated with Adamism (Gumilyov's "manfully firm view of life") is notably lacking in most poems. The Acmeist preference for words suggesting weight and mass and texture, on the other hand, is evident in a great number of poems.

The heaviness of spirit, for example, is conveyed in terms of physical weight. "It is your burden I bear, a heavy one" (*Tvoyo nesu ya bremya, tyazholoe*),[6] "My arms long for the burden [of an infant lost to his mother]" (*Ruki toskuyut po noshe, BS 138*). A mood of longing and inescapable boredom is intensified by the "heavily turning arms [of a windmill]" (*tyazhko mashushchie ruki, BS 139*). The wearied poet has "heavy lids" (*tyazhelye veki tvoi, Ch 183*); "I cannot lift my tired lids when he speaks my name" (*Ya ne mogu podnyat' ustalykh vek, kogda moyo on imya proiznosit, Ch 205*).

As these selections suggest, there is in Akhmatova's poetry an infinite weariness which has much more in common with Symbolism and the Decadence than with Adamist affirmation. The word *tomit'* (to weary, to tire, to torment) and its various derivatives occurs with such frequency that it cannot escape notice, and is in fact one of Akhmatova's minor motifs. Closely allied to this motif of infinite weariness is the idea of suffocation, of stifling atmosphere. *Dushno* (stifling) and its derivatives are also typical for Akhmatova's lexicon. The suggestion of physical weight is quite often employed in connection with these concepts.

In poems of a less somber tone, words suggestive of lightness, buoyancy, are used: "just before spring, there are such days, and the body is amazed at its lightness" (*Pered vesnoy byvayut takie dni/I lyogkosti svoey divitsya telo*). "The sky flew upwards; light are the outlines of things" (*Vysoko nebo vzletelo,/legki ochertaniya veshchey*). "My plume grazed the carriage top" (*Pero zadelo o verkh ekipazha, Ch 175*) opens a poem and sets the mood for the delicately restrained emotions of an Edwardian ride through the Bois de Boulogne.

Feathers, dust-motes in a sunbeam, tiny clouds like squirrel pelts spread out for curing: such images suggesting lightness occur typically in the rare poems dedicated to the joy of love; stones, however, are almost thematic. They occur typically in metaphors like the following; their weight is associated with heaviness of heart: "And a stone word fell upon my still living breast" *(I upalo kammenoe slovo/Na moyu eshchyo zhivuyu grud')*. The oppressive sky is a stone vault (P 83), the path of an abandoned woman is stony (BS 119); even the chill wind comes from the Stone Age *(veter kamennogo veka,* BS 115). "Fifteen years—feigned being fifteen granite centuries" *(Pyatnadtsat' let—pyatnadtsat'yu ve-kami/Granitnymi kak budto pritvorilis'),* "and I myself was like granite."

If love is lost, the living woman is but a finely chiseled statue; more than once the image of turning to stone is used. "And there my marble twin" *(A tam moy mramorny dvoynik,* V 225) implies the identification which is explicit in "Lot's Wife," who turned to a pillar of salt *(I sdelalas' prozrachnoyu solyu).* "I've got lots to do today:/ ... I've got to turn my heart to stone ..." *(U menya segodnya mnogo dela .../, Nado chtob dusha okamenela.)*

Mandelstam, who entitled one of his collections simply *Kamen'* (Stone), envisioned Akhmatova in this way:

> *In that half-turn, oh, the sadness!*
> *She looked upon the uncaring.*
> *Slipping from her shoulders,*
> *A neo-classical shawl turned to stone.*

> *The ill-boding voice—the bitter*
>   *intoxication—*
> *Unfetters the depths of the soul;*
> *Thus, an indignant Phèdre—*
> *Did stand, once, Rachel.*[7]

Mandelstam suggests the classical restraint of emotion in Akhma-tova's poetry with his first line, and prepares for the image of a marble statue in the Neo-Classical manner. The figure is solitary, as though removed from life by the tragedy of an ill-fated passion; it is the figure of a woman loving and unloved, ennobled by suffering, a portrait of Rachel in the role of Phèdre.

Like Mandelstam, Akhmatova makes use of stone as part of an architectonic mass. The oppressive sky, as noted above, becomes a stone vault; in a poem with a lighter mood, the sky is an "airy vault" (*svod vozdushny,* V 238). The arch of a burial vault (*arka sklepa,* V 237), barely glimpsed at the end of an *allée,* is an evil portent. The arch of a bridge (*pod ... svodom mosta,* Ch 189) is part of a whole complex of architectural images connected with the motif of Russia's cities. The detail of Petersburg's bridges occurs seemingly unconsciously in Akhmatova's poetry (AD 62, 64; BS 124, 131, 163, Ch 189), and the city itself seems to emerge through the brief glimpses of its churches, columns, and spires.

It is interesting to note that while the architectural imagery of the city draws on specific details of well-known buildings, the imagery connected with Akhmatova's symbolic "house" tends to the generic rather than the specific. The word *dom* (house) is a quite frequent one in Akhmatova's lexicon, and it occurs typically without distinguishing characteristics. The meaning of the Russian word is less precise than in English; it can mean "habitation" or even simply "building," as well as "house" or "home." Unlike the interior settings, where details are often specific and unusual, the details of the house itself are of the simplest and most general: door, window, threshold. The house imagery functions on the symbolic level rather than to suggest the Acmeist world of weight, mass, and line.

Even when images are employed which definitely suggest Acmeist concreteness, they occur characteristically without descriptive epithets. Textures are not described, but are suggested by the very essence of the object named. Akhmatova's stones are neither rough nor smooth, they are just stones. When descriptive epithets are employed, they are generally so much a part of the quality of the object that they scarcely represent modification at all—"soft" morocco leather, for example, or "red" wine.

I *Reification*

The tendency to concrete imagery extends even to abstractions, which are given attributes of material things, personified, or turned into concrete objects (the device of *oveshchestvlenie,* "reification," to use Vinogradov's word). [8]

In the poem "Progulka" ("The Ride", Ch 175), evening and sadness are made heavy in the literal sense, like iron, by the suggestion that they can be welded together (*Bezvetren vecher i grustyu skovan,* "Windless the evening and welded with grief"). Silence itself becomes an animate thing (*Benzina zapakh i sireni,/Nastorozhiv-shiysya pokoy,* "The smell of gasoline and lilacs,/The watchful silence"). In another poem a memory is like a stone at the bottom of a well: "Like a white stone in the depth of a well/There lies within me one memory" (BS 165).

Emotions and abstract ideas are transferred from the abstract realm to a more concrete one through physical action, as in the second line of the following example. "They fall in love" is rendered: "They wait for meetings, they fear partings,/They sing love songs" (BS 159).

"To pretend to be happy": "The orchestra is playing something gay/And my lips smile" (Ch 211).

"To be confused, in turmoil": "I drew my left-hand glove/Onto my right hand" (V 233).

"You feign tenderness": "In vain do you carefully wrap/My shoulders and breast in furs . . ." (Ch 184).

Not only are physical actions used to convey emotions and abstractions, but the word "body" itself occurs quite often and in a rather unusual way. It is substituted for the abstract *dusha* (soul): "And the body is amazed by its lightness" (BS 148). One would expect the word to read *dusha;* similarly, where "heart" or "soul" might be expected, "body" is employed in this instance: "My body is no longer festive" *(I uzhe ne prazdnuet telo)*. The physical sense of "heart" has been so displaced, in poetry at least, by the figurative sense that the word is too abstract for Akhmatova.

The concreteness of the physical world was, in Acmeist theory, closely associated with the plastic arts. Gumilyov had proceeded from Gautier's *Art Poétique* and its metaphor of painstaking sculpture and careful artisanry. Comparison with the plastic arts suggests itself in the poetry of Gumilyov and Zenkevich, as does architecture in Mandelstam and painting in Narbut and Gorodetsky. If such comparisons are valid, the one to be made with Akhmatova's lyrics is the one which she herself suggests: "As though sketched in India ink/In an old album was the Bois de Boulogne . . ." (Ch 175), and again "As though touched with black/Thick India ink are your heavy lids . . ." (Ch 183).

The compression of the following lines recalls the few economical brush strokes of the black and white wash drawing: "There's a kind of smile I have./Just a barely visible movement of the lips . . ." (Ch 186).

II *Color and the Seasons of the Year*

The delicacy and restraint typical of the line drawing are typical also of Akhmatova's lyrics, and the black and white coloration is suitable to the predominantly sad poems. It is interesting to note that Akhmatova's use of black and white, and indeed color in general, has much in common with Innokenty Annensky's. Both poets seem to use colors other than black and white principally in poems of a lighter mood.

The word white is omnipresent: white house, white columns, white yacht, white stone, white net of frost. The epithet is often applied in an extraordinary way: *"bely, bely Dukhov den' "* (White, white, All Soul's Day, BS 160), and *"belaya"* appears to signify death *(belaya smert');* the threshold of Paradise is white.[9]

Frequent as the epithet is, however, it is rarely obtrusive and never tires the reader: it is hardly noticed; one is not disturbed by the lack of color in an ink sketch. By the same token, black is used as effectively: black contagion, black wing of death, black ulcer, black beggarwoman.

The suggestion of black-on-white is often made without the use of these words: *snezhnaya noch* (snowy night), for example, or, in a description of a wintry, snow-covered Petersburg, "The wind, heavy and severe/Sweeps down soot from black chimneys" (Ch 209).

Some lines cited earlier in a different connection might be recalled in this context: "Children fed the speckled, greedy ducks/That bobbed in the inky icehole" (AD 64).

Akhmatova's city is most often seen with its granite dark against the winter's snows. On the darkened Moyka, snowy dust suddenly shines silver in a moonbeam; in another poem, snowflakes sparkle in the light of carriage lamps (AD 57); a house stands on a snowy corner (AD 62); the iceflow begins in the black Neva (BS 117); icebergs pass (P 76), and "In white hoarfrost, black firs/Stand on the melting snow" (BS 129).

Snow-whiteness is frequently used divorced from winter; lines of ink spread across a snow-white copy-book; a lover's breast is whiter than snow.

Winter is the favorite season, as the preceding examples indicate. In poems which are fixed in time and space, seasons pass, and a sense of chronology is felt in each volume, indeed in all six of the

volumes which belong to the period considered. A marked sense
of the passage of time is created, and with it the waiting, the expectation, and ultimately, the despair. A whole year's turning of
the seasons is encompassed in a brief poem of but twelve short lines
(BS 119). It opens with the heroine's dream on Christmas Eve,
that magical dream at Christmastide, which in Russian folk tradition promises love and shows the face of the future lover. From
mid-winter, time moves to spring; the peal-bearing winds of Easter
carry hope—if now wavering—in the promise of the winter's dream.
Abruptly it is summer, summer with its dragonflies on the rusted
iron of a fence, and the realization that the winter's dream will
never be fulfilled.

In Akhmatova's poetry, summer is not the time of happiness;
the brightness of its days is the blankness of despair. Spring brings
deceit and betrayal; autumn is, after the summer's despair, a meek
and quiet resignation to a life with only the memory of love. "There
is a fifth season; sing only its praises" (*To pyatoe vremya goda;
tol'ko ego slavoslov'*, BS 149). The fifth season is love, and only
there is happiness assured. If happiness occurs, however momentarily, in earthly time, then it is most likely to occur in winter.

Thus, Akhmatova's use of the seasons is in a way opposite to that
of Western literary tradition. It is not, however, unique in Russian
poetry, but follows a convention established in the early nineteenth
century with Vyazemsky and Pushkin. In this convention, winter
is not symbolic of old age, of sleep or suspension of life; rather it
is the season of freshness, renewal and revitalization—a time for
young love. Summer is, according to the convention, "but a car-
icature of Southern winters," in the words of Pushkin.[10]

In another poem there is a closely parallel structuring on the
symbolism of the seasons (V 230). Here, instead of the Christmas
dream, there is the *gadanie* (fortune telling) at Christmastide. A
maiden may foresee her future by going through certain rituals;
the face of the lover may appear in a looking glass. In this poem,
the heroine foresees her lover in December, and in January she is
his. But her happiness can last only through the winter; in spring she
must be abandoned. Her lover asks, "Isn't it a pity that your body/
Will melt in March, my fragile snowmaiden?"[11]

Shadings of the primary colors are quite atypical and the primary colors themselves, when employed, are usually so much a
property of the object modified that they are scarcely modifiers at

all: "red" wine, for example, or "blue" sky, or "red" maple leaf, or "grey" dove. (The last example, *sizy golub,* has a fixed epithet from the folk tradition; it is in this tradition that Akhmatova uses it.)

The only primary color which is sufficiently employed as to indicate a conscious device on the part of the poetess is the color yellow. As Gumilyov noted in his "Letter" on Akhmatova's *Rosary,* it is a most unusual color in poetry, perhaps the least employed. It is used at only one point in the black-and-white composition, suggesting comparison with the monochromatic Japanese print or wash drawing, where the yellow lamps of pilgrims on the Tokaido provide a focal point on the dark background, or where a single lighted window shines in a darkened Kyoto street.[12] Typical of this manner is the "Song of the Last Meeting," in which the heroine, rejected, returns alone to her darkened house, where "Only in the bedroom candles burned/With an indifferent-yellow light."

As in this instance, the application of the color epithet is often extraordinary. A memory is yellower than dead grass (V 229); from the pain of love, the heroine becomes yellow and faltering (P 85). The color often carries the connotation of a heavy and oppresive atmosphere: *zhyoltoy lyustry bezzhiznenny znoy* (BS 132) (the lifeless heat of the yellow chandelier)." Compare the effect of the color and of the sounds in this example: *I nad gorodom zhyoltuju mut'* (Ch 199) ("And above the city a yellow turbidness"). Against a fresh winter's background, where the Lebyazhya lies in crystals and the Champ de Mars in great icebergs, the contrast is provided by the yellow doors of a steaming livery stable.[13]

It is significant that the materials which Akhmatova chooses for her weight-mass suggestion have colors proper to them which are close in quality to black, white, or (more rarely) yellow. Bitter laughter is bronze *(Sem' dney zvuchal to medny smekh);* weeping is silvery *(To plach struilsya serebristy,* BS 110). Gold and gilt are frequent, especially in connection with architectural detail. A heavy, close day is "amber" *(On dlitsya bez kontsa, yantarny, tyazhky den',* BS 192). The black, cast-iron fences of Petersburg are a kind of leitmotif in Akhmatova's poetry, symbolizing the city.

In art, the *blanc-et-noir* technique has the delicacy, refinement and restraint typical of Akhmatova's verse, but the parallel does not suggest its energy, force, and highly charged passion. Marina

Tsveraeva conveys the profound emotional effect of Akhmatova's poems by employing herself the black-on-white medium.

Lines to Akhmatova

O Muse of tears, most splendid of the Muses!
O thou, crazed child of the white night!
A black blizzard wilt thou send onto Rus,
And thy wails pierce us like arrows.

. . . Anna
Akhmatova! That name is an immense sigh,
And it falls into depths which are
 nameless.   *(1916)*[14]

III *Verbal Economy*

Akhmatova's extreme economy in the use of color epithets, compared, for example, to Gorodetsky, Narbut, or Gumilyov, is typical for her use of descriptive epithets in general. We have earlier noted that textural epithets, modifying the concrete objects used as images in Akhmatova's poetry, are very sparingly employed. Adjectives are comparatively few; adverbs and verbal modifiers are preferred, and in comparison with most other poets, similes and metaphors are minimal.[15] The utter starkness of the "black blizzard" of Akhmatova's poems derives not only from her use of color, but from the directness of syntax, the avoidance of "poetic" vocabulary, turns and *ukrasheniya* ("decoration"), and the unembellished conversational style. Through simple forms and familiar images, Akhmatova achieves an unusual pathos in the expression of what she called the "wonderfully-simple," universal themes of a woman's love. The following illustrative tercet is the last selection in *Rosary:* "Will you forgive me these November days./In the canals off the Neva lights are sundered./Poor is the finery of the tragic autumn."

The compression and energy of expression illustrated here were considered by Eykhenbaum to be the basic traits of Akhmatova's poetry.

Despite the directness and verbal economy, however, there is inherent in Akhmatova's lexicon a richness and splendor which has nothing to do with exotic vocabulary, obscure literary references, or *recherché* metaphor. The words which impart opulence and lavishness to the studied plainness of the simple fabric are not merely applied but are integral to the design, for these words are organic to Akhmatova's subthemes. Nor are they to be separated from the simple, ordinary words—gloves, a muff, a windowsill, a doorstep—which are so characteristic and meaningful in Akhmatova's poetry. To the *personae* of her poems, these everyday words are not distinct from that part of the lexicon which gives fullness, depth, solemnity, and sometimes even majesty to the brief and highly personal lyrics.

Under the dominant of love, the subthemes to which this part of Akhmatova's lexicon is proper are the subthemes of Old Russia, of Russian Orthodoxy, of the Russian folk, of the ancient cities and limitless countryside of her homeland. The rich and varied historical and cultural associations with these subthemes are not presented so much in opposition to the contemporary concerns of the *persona* as they are presented as part and parcel of her consciousness.

Thus, for the *personae* of Akhmatova's poems, words such as *epitrakhil* (the long stole of the Orthodox priest), *emalevy obrazok* (small enamel icon), *panikhidy* (solemn funeral rites), *postnik* (one who fasts), do not represent a lexicon of religious exoticism, but are ordinary words from her everyday life. Similarly, the folk and Old Russian motifs are the property of Akhmatova's *personae*, as part of a cultural inheritance. The cupolas of the cathedrals of Kherson and the battle of Kulikovo Field do not indicate the fashionable Medievalism of Akhmatova's early contemporaries, but are perceived only as background, enriching but not overwhelming the major motif.

If such cultural and historical images lend a dignity and a further dimension in depth to otherwise simple love lyrics, they never appear inappropriate or out of place, for they are as much a part of the tradition in which Akhmatova was nurtured as were the literary soirées and the pre-Revolutionary intellectual society of St. Petersburg.

The sense of history is strong in Akhmatova. Not only do her fragile love lyrics evoke the great Russian past, but they are a kind of poetic chronicle of the cataclysmic events of the decade 1912–1922. If national reminiscence has become a major motif in Akhmatova's recent work, her poems of this fateful decade register directly her contemporary Edwardian world—and its total destruction.

CHAPTER 7

Later Works

Anna Akhmatova entitled the last collection of her works *The Course of Time (Beg vremeni)*. Studiedly unassuming, like all her titles, this one is particularly significant. The collection includes poems from the six early books, and an entirely new one, called simply *The Seventh Book (Sedmaya kniga)*, containing works up to 1964. Where there is change—as expected of a talented poet over a fifty-five year period of creativity—there is also a quite remarkable continuity in *The Course of Time*. Akhmatova's sense of history, so important to the richness of the background in the early poems, becomes dominant and highly productive in the later works.

Where historical and cultural impressions were in the early poems fused with the intensity of the lyrical moment, in later works the historical moment itself is often the source of the lyrical emotion. The poet's past, already bound in the early books, and Russia's past, already an integral part of them, are the subjects of many of the more successful later works.

In style as well as theme, there is also a marked consistency. There is development, of course, a shift in emphasis, further experimentation—but it is difficult to find a poem from the later years which is not, in some important way, prefigured by the poetry of 1912–22. It is in this sense that one can agree with Akhmatova's recent critic, E. Dobin: "There was no early Akhmatova. A mature poet appeared before her readers, a poet with her own themes, her own intonations, and her own firmly chosen position."[1]

It is clear that Akhmatova herself felt the body of her work to be a unity. She did not hesitate to incorporate poems of an early date into collections of later poems, to remove poems from one collection and include them in another, or to rearrange excerpts from some works, written many years apart, into new ones. She even suggested that a study of her entire production could profitably be undertaken through an analysis of *The Poem Without a Hero*, completed only in 1962.

Thus, the feeling of continuity is strong. Judging from the volume *The Reed (Trostnik),* as it appears in *The Course of Time,* one could say a great deal about continuity and rather little about change. *The Reed* contains selections from the period of enforced silence, 1922–40. Akhmatova bitterly resented the critics who maintained that she had "stopped writing" during this period and one senses that there are a great number of poems which might have been included here, but were not. The collection is not so much of a piece as the earlier ones (which were written in comparatively short periods of time), nor does it have the internal unity of cycles that the *Seventh Book* has. The poems which do appear from the 1920's and early 1930's show no radical departure from those in the earlier collections. The art of poetry, Pushkin, the pain of love, Russia's cities—all these themes repeat themselves in the familiar forms, and could, without difficulty, be included in the other volumes. (As a matter of fact, some poems from this work, earlier entitled *Iva (The Willow)* were transposed to *The Seventh Book.*)

The most obvious failing of *The Reed,* presented as representative of the years of Akhmatova's first "silence," is omission of the long poem, *Rekviem (Requiem).* It is clear that the reason for its not being published in the Soviet Union is extraliterary: it deals with the Stalinist Terror. The two excerpts which appear in *The Reed* lose the extraordinary force which they have as part of the longer work.

Another result of the omission of *Requiem* is that *The Reed* gives no indication of the beginnings of notable change in the "Akhmatova style." In the late 1930's, Akhmatova was haunted by the poem *Requiem,* and by 1940, was able to complete most of it. In December of that year, Akhmatova conceived and wrote the central part of *Poem Without a Hero.* Thus, the two major works were begun in that one year, an outstanding one in the continuum of Akhmatova's career.

> *From the year 1940,*
> *As from a tower, I look upon everything.*
> *As though I were bidding farewell again*
> *To that which I'd long since bid farewell,*
> *As though I had crossed myself,*
> *And walk off under dark vaults.*
> ("Introduction," *Poem Without a Hero*)

The Seventh Book, representing the post-1940 period, shows many of the tendencies exhibited in one or the other of the long poems. The tendency to greater length is observed, for example in "Pre-History" (1945), which is one Akhmatova's most successful later poems; and there is a trend toward length in the grouping of shorter poems into discreet cycles.

In the poems of greater length, too, there is a tendency to draw on the general, European cultural and literary traditions, rather than the almost strictly Russian associations characteristic of much of the earlier poetry. Together with this there is a greater intellectual weight than Akhmatova chose to give the early works.

Apart from these generalizations, it is difficult to draw comprehensive comparisons between *The Seventh Book* and the earlier production. With regard to versification and technical questions, for example, one might note the preference for a more strict meter for certain purposes—but this technique was well worked out in the early period. One might note the tendency away from the real world toward unreality, mirror images and dreams—but this, too, is foreshadowed in the early work. Similarly, the famous "clarity" associated with Akhmatova is not typical of some later works— but there are early works, like "The Bonfire" "Kostyor" for example, which are anything but "clear." Moreover, there are some late poems which could easily fit into *The Rosary* and even the first volume, *Evening* [e.g. "Do not threaten me with a terrible fate/ And a great northern longing . . ." (1959)]. It is thus very difficult to make other than heavily qualified generalizations about any "changes" in Akhmatova's poetry, beyond those few mentioned above.

It is not within the scope of this chapter to present a close comparison of the works in *The Seventh Book* with the volumes preceding. It is possible, however, to characterize the two major works of the later period, which represent, despite the continuity, the most distinct departure from the early lyrical works.

Akhmatova had experimented with the longer form before: *At the Very Edge of the Sea* (1914), and a *skazka,* or folk tale in the manner of Pushkin, "The Tale of the Black Ring" (1917). These works are strictly narrative poetry (both on the early theme of the lost lover), and have very little indeed in common with *Requiem and Poem Without a Hero.* Only in the poem, *1916 (Shestnadtsaty god),* do we find a poem of some length sharing characteristics with these two poems: and it, significantly, was written in the same year of 1940.[2] None of the poems is strictly narrative; they are made up of distinct parts which vary widely in length, versification and style; each poem is built on the tension between the deeply lyrical and an almost epic quality; there is a juxtaposition of personal loss and national tragedy. The three poems are set on the eve of the most violent dislocations Russia has known in this century.

A close analysis of these three poems would represent a major critical study in its own right; it is possible here only to give some idea of the nature of the two masterworks, *Poem Without a Hero* and *Requiem*. The "Petersburg Tale" in *Poem Without a Hero* carries the title "1913": that "last year," the final year of peace, the end of the Edwardian world, the eve of the First World War. The poem was conceived at the end of 1940, on the eve of World War II, and the final section ends[3] with Russia retreating to the East before the German armies. The poem *1916*, is about Russia at war, and the year is the eve of the Revolution. *Requiem* was composed at the end of the Stalinist Terror, and in the year before German troops overran Russia.

I Poem Without a Hero

In the sense of history and time, *Poem Without a Hero* is the most comprehensive, and any discussion of Akhmatova's later poetry must include some commentary on at least the nature of this remarkable work. It is a puzzling one. The first and major part—"1913: A Petersburg Tale"— is accessible on first reading only to the few surviving contemporaries who knew the narrow, but exciting world of Russian art and letters before the First World War. It is a private poem, a laying to rest of old ghosts, an exorcism of present terrors, a catharsis. Akhmatova wrote: " . . . Someone even suggested that I make the poem more understandable. I shall refrain from that . . . I shall neither change it nor explain it. *Ezhe pisakh—pisakh.*"[4] And in a letter to a friend, Akhmatova admitted candidly that " . . . to those who do not know the 'Petersburg circumstances' [of that time], the poem will be incomprehensible and uninteresting."[5]

Fortunately, Korney Chukovsky, a contemporary and an admirer of Akhmatova's verses since the early days, has unravelled

many of the riddles in his article, "On Reading Akhmatova."[6]
Further, Amanda Haight's notes to the final version authorized
by Akhmatova are most helpful.[7] These sources permit a fair
reading of the poem, although precise interpretation of certain
passages is still not possible.

Akhmatova once made a highly intriguing comment—without
elaboration—about the "Petersburg Tale." She called it a "polemics
with Blok."[8] The remark raises many interesting possibilities for
investigation, but the spare statement alone gives no inkling of
Akhmatova's intent.

Also puzzling is the very construction of the poem. "The Petersburg Tale" is a complete work in itself, and in itself, beautifully
structured. The next two parts, however, seem to have only tan-
gential relationships with it and with each other. Akhmatova
wrote of the problem: " . . . In the course of fifteen years, this
poem, like the attacks of some incurable disease, would suddenly
come upon me again and again . . . and I could not tear myself
away, adding to and correcting the obviously completed work."[9]

Whatever the problems engendered by the three-part work
(it is subtitled "Triptych"), "The Petersburg Tale" is a work of
great stature, and the entire poem may be, as Akhmatova's recent
critic E. Dobin has said, "one of the high points in Russian poetry."[10]

The genesis of the "Petersburg Tale" is an oddly simple one.
Bes poputal v ukladke rytsya, "The devil misled me into rummaging
about in my trunk" (Part II, *Reshka*); Akhmatova turned up a
tragic story from the now distant past:

> In the fall of 1940, straightening up my old papers (later lost during the
> Siege), I came upon some letters and poems, which had been with me long
> since, but which I had not read. They had to do with the tragic event of
> 1913 which is related in the *Poem Without a Hero.*[11]

The tragedy involved a very close friend of Akhmatova, Olga
Afanasievna Glebova-Sudeykina. She was a beautiful actress and
an accomplished dancer of the Suvorinsky Theater, the wife of a
recognized painter, a superlative hostess, and one of the most
fashionable ladies of Petersburg's artistic and intellectual society
in the years before the cataclysm. She was also an exquisitely sensitive person, and capable of great suffering.[12]

In 1913, a poet and cornet in the dragoons, twenty-year-old Vsevolod Knyazev, fell deeply in love with the famous actress. One night, he followed her to her home. She was not alone. The young man put a pistol to his forehead, and fell at the actress' very doorstep.

This, then, is the "Petersburg Tale." But it is not just the sad story of a foolish young dragoon and a beautiful actress. It is also partly the story of that "last year" 1913, partly Akhmatova's story ("my twin," she calls the actress in the poem), and partly the story of Petersburg society in that year before the end. There were masquerades and balls, carriages racing across the bridges, the Imperial Standard raised above the palace, the theater and the "Roving Dog," folly and foolishness and, in some, a frenetic search for escape:

> The holidays were warmed by the bonfires*
> And carriages plummeted from off the bridges,
> And the whole funereal city sailed
> On some unknown assignment
> Down the Neva or against the current—
> Only away from their own graves.

According to Boris Filippov, only the "eccentrics" like Akhmatova and Blok really sensed the approaching disaster. For the others, there was unclouded gaiety, frivolousness and a blissful unawareness.[13] To the "eccentrics" how unreal it all must have seemed.

In the "Petersburg Tale," Akhmatova does not "relate" the story of the young dragoon and the actress. Instead of the story, there is the event itself: one among others. It is scarcely symbolic— and yet there was in this purely personal tragedy something that might be generalized: the helplessness, the hopelessness, and even the foolishness of the act must have seemed to Akhmatova somehow characteristic of the age.

Like Pushkin's Parasha and Evgeny, the actress and the dragoon are juxtaposed in their personal tragedies with the blind force of historical events:

---

* Coachmen kept bonfires near the theaters and at street corners to keep warm until their masters returned.

> *The dénouement is ridiculously close;*
> *From behind screens, Petroushka's mask,*
> *The coachmen dance around their bonfires,*
> *Over the palace, a black-and-yellow banner . . .*
> *Everyone who needs to be is in his place;*
> *From the Summer Garden comes the scent*
> *Of the fifth act. . . . The phantom of the hell*
> *At Tsushima is here, too.—A drunken sailor*
> *Sings.*

Thus, the "Petersburg Tale" is also the tale of a historical moment; as Korney Chukovsky observed, in his article "Reading Akhmatova," perhaps the real hero of the *Poem Without a Hero* is Time:

> *The wind tore posters from the wall,*
> *Smoke danced a gopak on the roof,*
> *And the lilacs smelled of the graveyard.*
> *And accursed by Tsaritsa Avdot'ya,**
> *Dostoevskian and demoniac,*
> *The city went off into its fog.*
>
> . . .
>
> *An incomprehensible roaring hid there. . . .*
> *But at the time it was scarcely heard,*
> *It hardly even touched the hearing*
> *And drowned in the snowbanks on the Neva.*
>
> . . .
>
> *And along the legendary embankment*
> *Comes not the new century by calendar,*
> *But the real Twentieth Century.*

If Akhmatova does not "relate" the story of the dragoon and the actress, neither does she "recreate" the Petersburg of 1913. What she creates is her sense of the time—the feeling of apprehension, impermanence and unreality. The "characters" are shades and shades of shades, masks, mirror images, portraits stepping from their frames, figures perhaps glimpsed in darkened windows. It is a shadow-play, a "hellish harlequinade," a "Hoffmaniana"—a Symbolist's, not an Acmeist's Petersburg. The ghosts of the past swarm unbidden before the poet ·and are finally laid to rest. The "Petersburg Tale" is ended.

---

* Eudoxia, first wife of Peter the Great.

Still, the *Poem* will not let go. An "Intermezzo" follows. The time is the present (1941 and after) with the memory of the decades since 1913. "And the decades pass:/Wars, deaths, births—sing,/As you must see, I cannot."

These three lines are preceded by three omitted ones and followed by two stanzas omitted entirely, but indicated by stanza number and lines of dots. This, Akhmatova said, was in imitation of Pushkin.[14] Some indication of Akhmatova's incredibly difficult life during these years might have filled these stanzas, but complaints about her personal circumstances in regard to the authorities have no place in her poetry. The omitted lines are eloquent enough.

The "Intermezzo" is, in part, a literary causerie about the conception of the poem, about its composition, and, in an indirect way, about the difficulties with the publishers (censors). The poet and his work, the Poet and the Crowd—these are Pushkin's themes and the "Intermezzo" begins with a light irony that is Pushkin-like, and recalls Pushkin's satirical piece, "Conversation of a Bookseller with a Poet." Here, in Akhmatova's work, the poet speaks with a Philistine editor, who grumbles: "... There are three themes at once here!/When you've read the last line/You can't understand who's in love with whom."

Akhmatova must have intended a parallel to be drawn between her own situation and Pushkin's in regard to the censors and the "booksellers." The last part of Pushkin's "Conversation" is especially relevant:

> *The Bookseller*
>
> . . .
> *And so, wearied by love,*
> *Bored with the prattle of talk,*
> *You have rejected too early*
> *Your inspired lyre.*
> *Now, having abandoned noisy society,*
> *The muses, and fickle fashion,*
> *What then will you choose?*

> *The Poet*
> *Freedom.*
> *The Bookseller*
>
> *Fine. Here's some advice for you;*
> *Attend to this useful truth:*

> *Our age is a sharp trader; in this iron age*
> *There is no freedom without money.*
>
> . . .
>
> *I foresee your objection;. . .*
> *Your creation is dear to you,*
> *While in the flame of work*
> *The imagination boils and rages;*
> *But it will grow cold, and then*
> *Your piece grows cold to you also.*
> *Let me tell you simply:*
> *Inspiration does not sell,*
> *But you can sell a manuscript.*[15]
>
> . . .

In Pushkin's satire, the poet sells the manuscript. Akhmatova does not maintain the lightly satirical tone of her first stanzas. She will not compromise—and will continue to write according to her artistic conscience.

> *I agree to failure*
> *And I do not hide my agitation—*
> *My work box has a triple bottom.*
>
> . . .
>
> *And I write in mirror writing,*
> *There is no other road for me—*
> *By a miracle, I hit upon this one,*
> *And am in no hurry to leave it.**

The difficult road is taken. The poet agrees to lack of success, and does not even speak of the pain and hardship the choice entails. She will write as she wills, not as she is told.

The "Epilogue," or Part III, returns to Peter's city, this time in the present (1942), when Leningrad lay in ruins and Akhmatova was far away from it—evacuated during the siege to Tashkent. The "Epilogue" is dedicated "To My City," and begins with a farewell to it. As the Russian army fell back before the German offensive it seemed that all Russia was going into exile.

Although Akhmatova continued work on the *Poem* for another twenty years, it is at this indecisive historical moment that she

---

* Stanzas XVI and XVII, "Intermezzo," *Poema bez geroya.*

fixed for the ending of the "Epilogue": an open point in time, with no finality such as the end of the war or the return to Leningrad. The sense is not of history past, but of time in an unending continuum. The poem ends—and does not end—with these lines: "And wringing her hands, Russia/Marched before me to the East."

This suspension, rather than the finality of a different kind of conclusion, [16] may be unsatisfying, but it suits Akhmatova's purpose in her new conception of time.

> *As the future ripens in the past,*
> *So does the past moulder in the future.*

These lines, which are central to the *Poem Without a Hero*, might serve as an epigraph for a collection of the later poems, including the other major work undertaken in that same year of 1940: *Requiem*.

II Requiem

Unlike the *Poem Without a Hero*, *Requiem* is not a private poem. It is not so much a new experiment in Akhmatova's poetry as a culmination of a style perfected over the decades preceding; Akhmatova organizes her characteristic devices and techniques into an amazingly powerful statement which requires no elaboration or "explanation."

Neither is the *Requiem* a private poem in the sense that the subject, unlike that of the "Petersburg Tale," is immediately accessible to anyone with a knowledge of Russia's recent history—and all too well-known to those who lived in Russia during the late 1930's. The poem is, if not private, deeply personal: but Akhmatova is able to generalize her own shattering experience into an epic cry for her people. It was a time when "The stars of death stood above us,/And guiltless Russia huddled trembling/Under bloody boots/ And under the tires of the Black Moriahs."

For the introduction to *Requiem*, Akhmatova wrote: "In the terrible years of the Ezhovshchina*, I spent seventeen months in the prison lines in Leningrad." Time has dulled the mind to the

---

* The "Ezhov time"; from N. I. Ezhov, head of the N.K.V.D. (Secret Police) from 1936–38, who led the Terror.

enormity of what happened in Russia in the late 1930's, but Akhmatova's contemporaries can recall the horror bound up in her simple statement.

After the murder of the Leningrad Party Secretary Sergey Kirov in 1934, there started a chain reaction of political arrests, interrogations and executions which climaxed in the Great Purge of 1935–38. The show trials and the liquidation of the "enemies of the people" began. The population of the prison camps grew from six million in 1937 to ten million by 1940–42.[17] Even ordinary and innocent people were denounced in the general hysteria. In the cities, the prisons filled the minds of everyone; scarcely a family was not in some way affected. Long lines of mothers, wives and sisters formed beneath the prison walls. It is here that Akhmatova stood, waiting for news of her imprisoned son, Lev; it is here that she raised her cry for Russia's suffering, and it is here she would have her monument raised:

> *And if someone in this land*
> *Thinks to raise a monument to me,*
>
> *I agree to this honor*
> *But with a condition—place it not*
>
> *Near the sea, where I was born,*
> *My last tie with the sea is broken,*
>
> *Nor near that sacred stump in the garden at Tsarskoe,*
> *Where an inconsolable shade searches for me,*
>
> *But here where I stood for three hundred hours,*
> *And where they did not draw back the bolts for me.*
>
> *Because, even in blessed death I'm afraid*
> *I'll forget the rumble of the Black Moriahs,*
>
> *Forget how the hateful door clanged shut,*
> *And how an old woman howled like a wounded beast.*

As part of the introduction, Akhmatova gives a brief reminiscence from the days spent in the prison lines:

Once somebody somehow "recognized" me. Then a woman behind me, lips blue from the cold, who had never before heard my name, wakened from the stupor common to us all and asked close to my ear (we all spoke in whispers there): "And you can describe this?" And I said, "I can." Then something like a smile slipped over what had once been her face.

It is to these women that Akhmatova dedicates her poem, and with their voices that she speaks:

> *I would like to name them all by name,*
> *But the list has been taken away and there's nowhere to find out.*
>
> *For them I wove a wide cover*
> *Out of the poor words I overheard from them.*
>
> *I remember them always and everywhere,*
> *And I shall not forget them even in some new sorrow.*
>
> *And if they shut my tortured mouth*
> *Which shouts with the voices of a hundred million,*
>
> *Let the women remember me likewise*
> *On the eve of my memorial day.*

These lines come from the "Second Epilogue"; the structural divisions in the poem are quite complex. There is the prose "In Place of an Introduction," a dedication, a poetic "Introduction," and then a series of ten lyrical poems, not directly related to one another, and employing a variety of styles and moods, but each representing a step in a progression which replaces the usual poetic narrative. The two epilogues follow, returning from the lyric to the epic stance of the "Dedication" and "Introduction."

The "Dedication" begins: *Pered etim gorem gnutsya gory,/Ne techyot velikaya reka*/(Before such grief mountains bend,/The great river does not flow).

Akhmatova's genius at orchestration makes the opening line a wonderfully powerful one.[18] The "Dedication" continues to state the theme of the poem, and the "Introduction" repeats it: "It was when only the dead/Smiled, glad to be at peace./And Leningrad, like a useless appendage,/Flapped beside its prisons."

From the general and epic tone of the prefatory pieces, the first poem of the cycle shifts to the specific and individual, a short lyric with the distinctive marks of Akhmatova's style:

> *They led you away at dawn;*
> *I walked behind you as in a funeral,*
> *The children wept in the darkened chamber,*
> *The candle at the shrine overflowed.*
> *On your lips, an icon-like coldness.*
> *Deathly sweat on your brow . . . not to be forgotten.*
> *And I like the wives of the Streltsy**
> *Will howl under the Kremlin's towers!*

The suggestion of a funeral is not an unusual one in Akhmatova's early poetry (compare from *1916* the lines: *ya plakal'shchits stayu vedu za soboy*—I lead behind me a flock of mourners).

Also, the rich lexicon borrowed from an older Russia is, as we have seen, a characteristic feature of Akhmatova's earlier work: the almost obsolete *gornitsa* (chamber), the Orthodox associations of the word *bozhnitsa* (shrine, perhaps icon stand or icon corner), and the comparison using the word "icon" itself.

The breathless hesitancy of the lyrical moment which marks so many of the early lyrics is here. At the full realization of the emotion, there is a breaking point; the melted wax on the votive candle trembles and spills over. The wire snaps; control is gone: *"Budu ya kak streletskie zhonki/Pod kremlyovskimi bashnyami vyt'!"/* (And I like the wives of the Streltsy/Will howl under the Kremlin's towers!)

This is an astonishingly forceful evocation of another tragic time in Russian history: the wives wailing near the walls of the Kremlin, their husbands executed before their eyes. Into this powerful image, Akhmatova introduces a note of pathos in the unexpected diminutive of "wives" *(zhonki)*. In the tension created, she has produced two of her most striking lines. The wail of the Streltsy women is echoed again in the "Epilogue"—in the howl of the old woman as the prison door slams shut on her loved one. There arises a whole series of associations with the brave and loyal Russian women who followed their men into prison and exile—from Nataliya Dolgorukaya to Maria Volkonskaya and beyond.

---

* The Streltsy were a standing infantry which sided with the Tsarevna Sophia against Peter the Great in an attempt to preserve their power and privileges. After their second rebellion in 1698, Peter executed over seven hundred of the Streltsy, and many of them were killed before the walls of the Kremlin.

After a complete emotional break in Akhmatova's poems, we have come to expect a quick return to calm. In the early lyrics, it is often the calm of resignation, or that brought on by force of will. In the later poetry, there is the suggestion of an unnatural calm, a calm that is not quite sane. It is as though the mind, to protect itself, loses touch with reality and its unbearable grief. The tendency in some early poems for the *persona* to stand aside and apparently observe herself as a separate person is even more marked in the later poetry. Here, the separation can become complete.

The second lyric has meaning in this sense: a calm with a suggestion of madness after intense grief, and the dissociation of the poet from herself.

> *Quietly flows the quiet Don,*
> *Into the house comes the yellow moon.*
>
> *Comes in with his hat cocked jauntily,*
> *The yellow moon sees a shadow.*
>
> *This woman is sick,*
> *This woman is alone*
>
> *Husband in the grave, son in prison,*
> *Pray for me a little.*

The shift from the emotional break in the first lyric is abrupt; quiet is introduced in one line. The evocation of the Don also suggests a kind of epic calm, and is part of the epic motif of Russia's mighty rivers: the unnamed "great river" and the misty Neva of the "Dedication," the quiet Don here, the swirling Yenisei, and at the very end, once more the Neva.

Calm is reestablished, but it is only apparent: the odd impression of the moonlight suggests the mind disordered by grief, and there is a confusion between first and third persons. In the following lyric, the confusion is resolved: the *persona* divorced entirely from the suffering self. "No, that is not I, that is someone else who is suffering./I couldn't suffer like that, and as to what happened—/ Let it be covered over with black cloths,/And let the lamps be carried out . . ./Night."

The gesture of covering here is not simply suggestive of covering the dead; there is a subtle use here of a mainly Orthodox association which is not infrequent in Akhmatova's verse. It carries the idea of comfort and protection. In the "Epilogue," Akhmatova wrote of the women standing in the prison lines: "For them I wove a wide cover/Out of the poor words I heard from them."

The word used for cover is *pokrov,* and the Orthodox association is with the veil of the Virgin, its comfort and protection.[19]

With the finality of the single word "night" of the last line, the poem draws to a complete stop. The next part takes up a theme which is to be central to *The Poem Without a Hero:* time past in the present. The young noblewoman and fashionable poetess of Petersburg in 1913 reappears momentarily standing "three hundredth or so" in the line under the grim walls of the Kresty prison. There are now three *personae* present, the same and yet not the same: the grief-stricken mother, the person speaking here who cannot bear to suffer so, and the "gay little sinner of Tsarskoye Selo."

> *You should be shown, you who loved to make fun of things,*
> *You who were the favorite of all your friends,*
> *The gay little sinner of Tsarskoe Selo,*
> *What will happen in your life—*
> *As three hundredth or so in line*
> *You will stand under the Kresty walls,*
> *And with your hot tear*
> *Burn through the New Year's ice.*
> *And not a sound—and how many*
> *Innocent lives are ending there . . .*

The next two poems are lyrical treatments of the poet's apprehension of her terror and despair. They are followed by the central poem of *Requiem,* wonderfully simple and deeply moving in its simplicity.

The Sentence

> *And the stone word fell*
> *Upon my still living breast.*
> *Never mind, I was ready after all,*
> *I'll manage somehow or other.*
>
> *I have lots to do today:*
> *I have to kill my memory utterly,*
> *I've got to turn my soul to stone,*
> *I've got to learn to live again—*

> *And if not . . . The hot rustle of summer*
> *Is like a holiday outside my window.*
> *For a long time I've had a presentiment of this*
> *Bright day and empty house.*

For the central poem in her long work, Akhmatova chooses restraint where one might expect a complete breakdown or histrionics. After all, the fifth poem in the cycle begins "For seventeen months I've been crying out,/I am calling you home./I have thrown myself at the feet of the hangman;/You are my son and the terror of my life."

In "The Sentence," however, there is extreme understatement, a simple, workaday vocabulary and tone. It is not simply epic calm in the face of tragedy, or a kind of resignation and acceptance. The intensity of the moment is increased many times by the pathetic effort of the will to overcome a grief that borders on madness.

In the context of all Akhmatova's poetry up to this point, the poet's very own familiar devices and symbols, already perfected in less tragic days, lend an extraordinary pathos. The conversational tone, the stone imagery, the suggestion of clairvoyance, the peculiar use of bright/radiant, the pervasive symbol of the empty or abandoned house—all these things were once, after all, the stock-in-trade of the "gay little sinner of Tsarskoe Selo." Their reappearance here subtly compounds the emotional charge of this "restrained" lyric.

An apostrophe to death follows: "You will come anyway—so why not now?" The *persona* will greet death in any form he chooses—even in "the little game which he himself invented, and with which everyone is familiar to the point of nausea": "That I may see the top of a blue cap*/And the superintendent pale from fear./It's all the same to me. The Yenisei swirls/And the polar star shines . . ."

The next poem and the last lyric in the series takes up directly the theme of madness, again with the suggestion of another person suffering:

---

*The blue cap *(golubaya shapka)* is meant to suggest the N.K.V.D.; the superintendent *(upravdom)* is a kind of concierge and also a minor functionary who manages the building.

> *Madness has already covered*
> *Half my soul with its wing,*
> *And gives to drink of a fiery wine*
> *And beckons into a dark valley.*

> *And I understood that*
> *I must lose the battle to it,*
> *Listening to my own raving*
> *As though it were someone else's.*

> .   .   .

The last part of the poem proper is entitled "Crucifixion." In the brief space of two quatrains, Akhmatova is able to generalize the intensely lyrical emotion of the preceding cycle of nine poems. To do this, she relies once again on the universality of the mother suffering for the son sentenced and persecuted. From the mother and son, the poem moves to the Mother and the Son:

> *A mighty choir of angels praised the hour,*
> *And the skies melted in fire.*
> *To the Father He said: "Why hast thou forsaken me!"*
> *And to the Mother: "Oh, do not weep for me . . ."*

> *The Magdalene struck her breast and sobbed,*
> *The beloved disciple turned to stone,*
> *But there, where the Mother stood silent*
> *No one dared even to glance.*

The poem ends with this brief and extremely effective generalization of human experience, and in the "Epilogues," the epic stance of the introductory poems is again assumed. In the second "Epilogue," the theme receives its final statement. The pounding, compelling amphibracs give the impression that no force can stay the completion of that statement. And when it is completed, the poet returns again to the motif of the great rivers of Russia, here as in the first part, to the Neva and its association with Pushkin, *The Bronze Horseman,* with Peter the Great and Russian history:

> *I tikho idut po Neve korabli.*
> And the ships go quietly along the Neva.

Conclusion

It is early in time for any attempt at a final assessment of Akhmatova's work, or for trying to define her place in the history of Russian poetry. Her influence—and example—continue as a productive force in the poetry of some of Russia's most outstanding young poets. Among them is a small group which was very close to Akhmatova during the last decade of her life. It is therefore quite possible that Akhmatova may one day be recognized not only for her own work, but also as a direct link between what has been called the "Silver Age" of Russian poetry and another flowering of Russian verse. She made the following observation in 1964, two years before her death: "Not long ago, there was a Silver Age of Russian poetry, and now there will be a golden one. I am not exaggerating. We have a great many young people who live only for poetry. They write excellent poems, but don't want to be published. Days at a time, whole evenings, all night long they argue about poetry, discuss poetry, recite poetry—just like it used to be, even more than it used to be! Have you read Brodsky? In my opinion, he is a remarkable poet, and almost entirely mature."[1]

In one poem from the later years, "The Last Rose," Akhmatova speaks of the freshness of the new poetry after a lifetime as a poet. The first lines reflect the trials of her career:

> *I am to pray on my knees with Morozova,**
> *To dance with Herod's stepdaughter,*
> *To fly away with the smoke from Dido's pyre,*
> *So I can go again to the stake with Joan.*
> *Oh Lord! You see how tired I am*
> *Of being resurrected, of dying, of living.*
> *Take from me everything, only let me feel*
> *Once again the freshness of this bright red rose.*

---

*Feodosiya Prokofevna Morozova (died 1672) was a noblewoman who was exiled from Moscow and imprisoned in a convent for clinging to her religious beliefs in a time of schism in Russian Orthodoxy.

It was this kind of freshness that Akhmatova herself had brought to Russian poetry some fifty years before; her sense for it was never to be lost.

Notes and References

Preface

1. According to Aleksey Surkov, chairman of the Commission on the Literary Heritage of Anna Akhmatova, some of the materials are scattered, and it is not clear whether all of them are in the hands of the various state literary agencies. ("Literaturnoe nasledstvo A.A. Akhmatovoy," *Literaturnaya gazeta,* 5/3/1968.) The first volume of a comprehensive collection has been issued in the West under the editorship of G.P. Struve and B. A. Fillipov: *Sochinenia* (Munich: Interlanguage Literary Associates, 1965).

Chapter One

1. For reasons given in the Preface, quotations from Akhmatova's poetry will be taken from the readily available *Izbrannye stikhotvorenia,* New York: Chekhov Press, 1952. Numbers in parentheses refer to the corresponding pages of this edition. The prose translations which follow the quotations are my own, and are intended to convey the literal meaning as closely as possible. In subsequent chapters, the initials preceding the page numbers indicate the original collections from which the poems are taken.

2. A. Akhmatova, "Korotko o sebe," *Stikhotvorenia* (Moscow: Goslitizdat, 1961), p. 5.

3. *Sirius* survived for only three issues, and was abandoned when Gumilyov's funds were exhausted. Akhmatova wrote in a letter dated 13 March 1907 [quoted in E. Gollerbakh, 'Iz Vospominany o N.S. Gumilyove," *Novaya russkaya kniga* 7 (1922), pp. 37–41: "Why has Gumilyov undertaken the *Sirius?* It surprises me, and puts me in an extraordinarily gay mood. How many misfortunes our Mikola has undergone and all in vain! Have you noticed that the contributors are almost all as famous and respected as I am? I think the Lord must have darkened his senses (nashlo na Gumilyova zatmen'e ot Gospoda). It happens." The first publication of Akhmatova's poetry in Russia was in *Zhurnal dlya vsekh.*

4. Nikolay Stepanovich Gumilyov was born 3 April (old style) 1886 in Kronstadt, into the family of a naval surgeon. The family moved to

Tsarskoe Selo that same year. Although Gumilyov was three years older than Akhmatova, he was behind his class and was not graduated until 1906.

5. Both selections are quoted in Nikolay Otsup's biographical sketch of Gumilyov. N. Gumilyov, *Izbrannoe* (Paris: Librairie des Cinq Continents, 1959), p. 112. Gumilyov was the subject of N. Otsup's doctoral dissertation.

6. In 1905, Gumilyov had already published his first book of poetry, *Put' konkvistadorov (The Path of the Conquistadors)*.

7. It is said that he was relieved of his post as director for having shielded several students who had taken part in political disturbances during the troubled period 1905–6.

8. See I. Annensky, "Oni," *Apollon,* No. 3, 1909.

9. Akhmatova, A., *op. cit., Stikhotvorenia,* p. 7. (Referred to, hereafter, by title only).

10. Gumilyov, N., *op. cit., Izbrannoe,* p. 121 (Referred to, hereafter, by title only).

11. Akhmatova was slight, darkly handsome, with angular but delicate features. There is a portrait of Akhmatova by Nathan Altman (reproduced in *Apollon* No. 1, 1916, p. 27). On the basis of this portrait, Ilya Ehrenburg did a sensitive, impressionistic verbal sketch of the poet (*Portrety russkikh poetov.* Berlin: Argonavty, 1922, pp. 7–9). Yury Annenkov's famous drawing of Akhmatova is reproduced in L. Strakhovsky, *Craftsmen of the Word* (Cambridge: 1946). There is also a portrait of her by Modigliani.

Gumilyov, it seems, could only be described as physically unattractive. Nikolay Otsup (who knew him only after 1918), noted that "his head was unusually elongated, as though squeezed by the accoucheur's forceps"; he was slightly cross-eyed and had a tendency to lisp (*Izbrannoe,* p. 8).

12. References to solitary childhood appear in the poems of both Akhmatova and Gumilyov. See, for example, Akhmatova's *U samogo morya* and the poem "Iva" (9), and Gumilyov's "Pamyat," the first poem in *Ognenny stolp.*

13. Gumilyov's teacher, Bryusov, was influenced by Hérédia's literary exoticism and heroism, and translated some of his works into Russian. Gumilyov's *Path of the Conquistadors* is strongly reminiscent of Hérédia, while his enacted escape to Africa most certainly must have been inspired by Rimbaud.

14. Vera Nevedomskaya, "Vospominania o Gumilyove i Akhmatovoy," *Novy Zhurnal* 38, 1954, p. 186.

15. As a Gymnasium student, for example, Gumilyov remained uninterested in and entirely removed from the events of 1905. Just two years before, however, he had been politically active and even agitated among the millers of Ryazan province. Gleb Struve, "Biografichesky ocherk," *Otravlennaya tunika* (New York: 1952), p. 47.

16. *Izbrannoe*, pp. 9–10.

17. The tentative suggestion here is that Gumilyov considered his skull deformed and was morbidly sensitive about it. Irina Odoevtseva rejects the suggestion categorically (Irina Odoevtseva, *Na Beregakh Nevy* (Washington: Kamkin, 1968), pp. 105–6.

18. *Siluety russkikh pisateley*, vol. 3 (Berlin: "Slovo," 1923), p. 235.

19. Nikolay Gumilyov, *Chuzhoe nebo*, Georgy Ivanov, ed. (Berlin: Petropolis, 1936), p. 5.

20. Georgy Ivanov, *Peterburgskie zimy* (New York: Chekhov Press, 1952), p. 216.

21. Zavalishin subscribes to this theory along with Ivanov. Vyacheslav Zavalishin, *Early Soviet Writers* (New York: Praeger, 1958), p. 42.

22. On the conflict between the personalities of Akhmatova and Gumilyov, and their married life together, see Odoevtseva, *Na Beregakh Nevy*, pp. 462–91. Odoevtseva presents Gumilyov's view. She does not claim biographical accuracy, and her work seems rather a *biographie romancée*, but the depth of attachment between the two strong-willed poets is made clear, as is the inevitability of conflict and final rupture.

23. *Izbrannoe*, p. 68. This poem first appeared in Gumilyov's third collection, *Chuzhoe nebo* (Foreign Skies), 1910–1912. In this poem, Gumilyov rather unkindly, but amusingly satirizes the *persona* of Akhmatova's poems. For both Akhmatova and Gumilyov, the poetic *persona* seemed to become integral to the real personality—and these *personae* were diametrically opposed. The above poem, written in the first year of the ill-fated marriage, prefigures the ultimate separation.

24. *Stikhotvorenia*, p. 8.

25. Nevedomskaya, *op. cit.*, "*Vospominania*," p. 182.

26. The first was *Evening*, written in 1911 before her marriage to Gumilyov and published in 1912.

27. Dmitrij Tschizewskij, *Russische literarische Parodien*, Heidelberger Slavische Texte (Wiesbaden: 1957), p. 53.

28. Nevedomskaya, p. 189. The memoirist is slightly mistaken here. Blok never visited the Gumilyovs. D. Maksimov, "Akhmatova o Bloke," *Zvezda* (1967) 12, p. 188. See also *Na Beregakh Nevy*, p. 476.

29. *Stikhotvorenia*, p. 7.

30. *Stikhotvorenia*, p. 7.

31. P. P. Rubens, "Rubens o svoey zhivopisi." (Pisma za 1608–1637, otryvki iz traktatov i drugie materialy.) Perevod i primechania A. Akhmatovoy i A. Aristovoy. V knige *Mastera iskusstva ob iskusstve*, vol. I (Moscow-Leningrad, 1937), pp. 447–504.

32. See Sergey Makovsky, *Na Parnase serebryanogo veka* (Munich: Tsop, 1962), p. 210ff.

33. For example, V. Bryusov, "Segodnyashny den' russkoy poezii," *Russkaya mysl'* (1912), VII ii, pp. 11–28; V. Chudovsky, "Po povodu

stikhov Anny Akhmatovoy," *Apollon* (1912) 5, p. 45; and Georgy Chulkov, *Nashi sputniki 1912–1922* (Moscow: izd. Vasileva, 1922), p. 73.

34. E. Anichkov, *Novaya russkaya poezia* (Berlin: izd. Ladyzhnikova, 1923), pp. 42–43.

35. This was not the first poem read by Akhmatova at the Tower, as Georgy Ivanov's highly romanticized account has it (*Peterburgskie zimy*, pp. 78–80); Akhmatova rejected Ivanov's work, and was irritated by the scholars who cited this particular passage about her introduction at the Tower. For a truer account, see E. Dobin, *Poezia Anny Akhmatovoy.* (Leningrad: Sovetsky Pisatel', 1968), p. 25.

36. In a review of the eighth edition of *Rosary* (*Kniga i Revolyutsia*, 7, 1922, p. 63), Innokenty Oksenov wrote: "It is with some trepidation that one opens *Rosary* nowadays—for this book is removed from our times by eight years of trial which have left little of what used to be. But one is immediately convinced that *Rosary* has not become outmoded even for us; that the freshness . . . is the same; that the book, having survived these terrible, fateful years, will remain in Russian poetry forever."

37. N. V. Nedobrovo, "Anna Akhmatova," *Russkaya mysl'* July 1915, p. 50. The *Bol'Shaya sovetskaya entsyklopedia* (1926 edition) recognized a particular "Akhmatova style" in Russian lyricism.

38. Marina Tsvetaeva, *Proza* (New York: Chekhov Press, 1953), p. 279. The admiration was a mutual one. Mandelshtam once told Tsvetaeva that Akhmatova carried a manuscript copy of one of Tsvetaeva's poems in her purse until it fell to pieces. Tsvetaeva called this "one of the great joys" of her life.

39. Of those who published reminiscences of this period in the married life of Gumilyov and Akhmatova, Georgy Ivanov and Sergey Makovsky seem to have known the young couple best. Both indicate resentment. Odoevtseva, however, denies any such resentment in *Na Beregakh Nevy*, p. 479.

40. The letters and articles are collected in N. S. Gumilyov, *Pis'ma o russkoy poezii* (Petrograd: Tsentral'noe kooperativnoe izdatelstvo, 1923).

41. Compare also: *Zapreshchaesh' pet' i ulybat'sya,/A molit'sya zapretil davno* (75); *Byl on revnivym, trevozhnym i nezhnym,/Kak Bozhie solntse menya lyubil,/A chtoby ona ne zapela o prezhnem,/On beluyu ptitsu moyu ubil* (99); *Luchshe b mne chastushki zadorno vyklikat',/A tebe na khriploy garmonike igrat'* (168).

42. *Izbrannoe*, p. 74. Compare "Devushke," p. 64; "Razgovor," p. 129, "Ot'ezzhayushchemu," p. 140, "Angel-Khranitel'," p. 63.

43. Gumilyov was commissioned by the Academy of Sciences as director of the expedition. Its purpose was to study Abyssinian tribes and to compile a collection of artifacts from East African Life. The collection was placed in a museum in Petersburg.

44. Gumilyov had enrolled as volunteer in the Life-Guard Uhlan Reg-

iment of Empress Alexandra Fyodorovna in August, 1914. He was twice awarded the Cross of St. George.

45. Georgy Ivanov, *Peterburgskie zimy,* p. 85.

46. Shileyko had worked closely with Gumilyov on the latter's translation of the Gilgamesh epic, and himself translated *Oryol i Zmeya* (From the Babylonian, *Vostok* No. 4, 1924, pp. 24–26. In *Vostok* No. 1, 1922, he had published *Rodnaya starina* (echoes of Babylonian poetry in the poems of Russian writers).

47. Also published in this year was Akhmatova's long poem *U samogo morya (At the Edge of the Sea),* her only departure from the lyric genre in this period. It is, as Marietta Shaginyan observed, rather a compilation of earlier themes than a new work. *Literaturny dnevnik* (Moscow-Petersburg: Krug, 1923), pp. 116–23.

48. Vladislav Khodasevich, *Literaturnye stat'i i vospominania* (New York: Chekhov Press, 1954), p. 394. See also, A. Akhmatova, "Mandelshtam; listki iz dnevnika," *Vozdushnye puti* IV (1965), p. 29, p. 38.

49. For example, K. Mochulsky, "Anna Akhmatova, *Anno Domini MCMXXI,*" *Sovremennye zapiski* No. 10, 1922, pp. 389–90. Mikhail Pavlov, *"Anno Domini MCMXXI* and *U samogo morya," Kniga i revolyutsia,* No. 3, 1922, p. 72. S. Sumsky, *"Anno Domini," Novaya russkaya kniga* No. 1, 1922, pp. 20–21. Also: Shaginyan, pp. 116–23.

In retrospect, Vyacheslav Zavalishin wrote: "After the Revolution, the near-idolatry in which Anna Akhmatova was held among the intelligentsia only increased with the appearance of each new volume in the brief series [ending with *Anno Domini*] which continued for a few years." *Early Soviet Writers* (New York: Praeger, 1958), p. 47.

50. Blok dedicated a poetic tribute to Akhmatova in 1913, "Krasota strashna," reprinted in Erikh Gollerbakh, *Obraz Akhmatovoy, Antologia* (Leningrad: Leningradskoe Obshchestvo bibliofilov, 1925). Tsvetaeva recalls this bon mot of Blok's which neatly expresses both his own and Akhmatova's attitude toward poetry: "Akhmatova writes poetry as though a man is watching her; you should write poetry as though God is watching you . . ." (Tsvetaeva, p. 392). In a critical article on Acmeism, Blok stated flatly that Akhmatova was the only good poet in the movement ["Bez bozhestva, bez vdokhnovenia (Tsekh Akmeistov)," *Sochinenia* II (Moscow: Goslitizdat, 1955), p. 367.] This article, written soon after the appearance of the Acmeist manifestoes in 1913, was not published until 1921, the year of Blok's death.

In a letter to Akhmatova in 1916, Blok suggests that his reading of Akhmatova's *U samogo morya* restored his faith in the value of poetry (Pis'mo Akhmatovoy, 14 March 1916, *Sochinenia,* Vol. II, p. 705).

51. Sergey Makovsky, "Nikolay Gumilyov po lichnym vospominaniam" *Novy zhurnal* (Sept. 1964), p. 178. Akhmatova was disturbed by the rumor, and it probably prompted her rather puzzling short biographical note on

Blok, in which she made it clear that they had met only a few times, and that their relationship had been quite formal [Anna Akhmatova, "Vospominania ob Al. Bloke," *Zvezda* (1967) 12, pp. 186–87.]

52. Otsup writes: "At the Smolensk Cemetery, where we had carried the casket of Blok, representatives of the most outstanding scientific and literary organizations agreed to go to the Cheka with a request for Gumilyov's release to custody." N. Gumilyov, *Izbrannoe,* N. Otsup, ed., (Paris: Librairie des cinq continents, 1959), p. 19.

53. *Peterburgskie zimy,* p. 78. Ivanov's dramatized account suggests the strength of Akhmatova's resolve. She apparently deeply resented those who emigrated.

54. R. Ivanov-Razumnik, *Pisatel'skie sudby* (New York: Literaturny fond, 1951), p. 28.

55. A summary of this criticism is given in Leonid Grossman, "Anna Akhmatova," *Sbornik Svitok* IV, 1926, p. 296. A polemical battle between such outstanding figures as Vinogradov and Eikhenbaum arose concerning the proper approach to Akhmatova's poetry. Each wrote a book maintaining his point of view. If Vinogradov's semantic-linguistic approach is extreme, Eikhenbaum's book remains the best work on Akhmatova in Russian.

See: V. V. Vinogradov, *O poezii Anny Akhmatovoy* (Leningrad: Izd. Foneticheskogo Instituta Yazykov, 1925).

B. Eikhenbaum, Anna Akhmatova: *Opyt Analiza* (Petersburg: Petropechat, 1923).

56. V. Chudovsky, "Akhmatova i Mayakovsky," *Dom Isskustv* 1920, p. 23.

57. Innokenty Oksenov, "Pis'ma o sovremennoy poezii," *Kniga i Revolyutsia,* 12 (1921), p. 18.

58. V. Lvov-Rogachevsky, *Noveyshaya russkaya literatura* (Moscow-Leningrad: izd. Frenkel', 1925), p. 280ff.

59. N. Osinsky, "Pobeg i travy," *Pravda* 148 (1922).

60. G. Lelevich, *Na literaturnom postu* (Moscow: Oktyabr', 1924), p. 119. Also to be found in *Na postu* 2–3 (1923). This article is excerpted in *Literaturnaya entsyklopedia.*

61. George Gorbachev, *Ocherki sovremennoy russkoy literatury* (Leningrad: Gozidat, 1924), p. 17.

62. V. Arvatov, "Grazhdanka Akhmatova i tovarishch Kollontay," *Molodaya gvardiya* 4/5 (1923), pp. 147–51.

63. Viktor Pertsov, "Russkaya poezia v 1946 godu," *Novy mir* 3 (1947), pp. 172–82.

64. Yuly Aikhenval'd, *Siluety russkikh pisateley* (Berlin: Slovo, 1923), pp. 279–93.

65. Gollerbach, *Obraz Akhmatovoy,* passim.

66. See Aleksandra Kollontay, "Voprosy zhizni," *Molodaya gvardia,*

2/9 (1923), pp. 164–72, and the article by Arvatov cited on the preceding page. Arvatov's approach is naively statistical, and his tone derisive. His summation: ". . . and so, a narrow, small boudoir poetry: love from the bedroom to the croquet court. And this is recommended reading for the workers!" It is interesting to note that Arvatov's main point was not entirely original: it had been made in 1914 by R. Ivanov-Razumnik in "Zhemannitsy: *Chetki* Anny Axmatovoy i *Pechal'noe vino* Very Inber," *Zavety* 5 (1914).

67. *Iz shesti knig* (Leningrad: Sovetsky pisatel', 1940).

68. *Pisatel'skie sudby*, p. 28.

69. A. Akhmatova, *Stikhotvorenia* (Moscow: Goslitizdat, 1961), pp. 300–301. It is interesting to note that in the summer of 1959 when I discussed Akhmatova's poetry with Surkov (then chairman of the Moscow Writers' Union), his attitude was quite different: he condemned Akhmatova's work *in toto,* categorically and heatedly. He has since, however, worked for the rehabilitation of Akhmatova (See Giancarlo Vigorelli, "La mia visita ad Anna Achmatova," *Sucesso,* September 1963, p. 119).

70. "O zhurnalakh *Zvezda* i *Leningrad:* iz postanovleniya TsK VKP (b) ot 14 Avgusta 1946 g; Doklad tovarishcha Zhdanova o zhurnalakh *Zvezda* i *Leningrad,*" *Sovetskaya kniga* (1946) No. 8–9.

71. One example of Zhdanov's rantings is sufficient to characterize the whole of his report: Akhmatova is "a representative of reactionary obscurantism and a political renegade . . . a representative of that idealess reactionary literary swamp, Acmeism, which wants to know nothing about the People . . ." Zhdanov speaks of Akhmatova's useless digging about in her own shallow soul, and says that the scope of her poetry is limited to the point of paucity—"the poetry of a noblewoman run amok, scuttling between bedroom and chapel . . . 'not quite a harlot and not quite a nun,' but surely more harlot than nun, in whom licentiousness is mixed with prayer."

As criticism alone, Zhdanov's report was not only intellectually dishonest, but stupid. In the above citation, he distorts a phrase of Eikhenbaum which had become a kind of critical tab for Akhmatova: ne to "bludnitsy" s burnymi strastyami, ne to nishchey monakhini (not quite a "harlot" with violent passions, not quite a poor nun; in *Opyt analiza,* p. 114). Zhdanov does not credit Eikhenbaum, and ignores his intent: to characterize a psychological tension which he felt Akhmatova used as a conscious literary device. For illustration of his point, Zhdanov most unfortunately chose the following lines, not realizing that both the construction and the juxtaposition were modelled on a passage from Lermontov's *Demon:* "No klyanus' tebe angel'skim sadom,/Chudotvornoy ikonoy klyanus'/ I nochey nashikh plammenykh chadom. . . ."

72. Along with Alexander Tvardovsky and Vera Inber, Pertsov was on the editorial board of the 1961 edition of Akhmatova's poems.

73. "Russkaya poezia v 1946 godu," *Novy Mir* (1947) 3, p. 178.

74. "Za vysokuyu ideynost' sovetskoy literatury," *Protiv bezideynosti v literature* (Moscow: Sovetsky Pisatel', 1947), pp. 16–17.

75. I. Sergievsky, "Ob antinarodnoy poezii Anny Akhmatovoy," in *Protiv bezideynosti v literature.* Compare also D. Danin, *Protiv bezideynosti i poshlosti* (O literaturnykh stranitsakh v gazetakh voysk Ministerstva vnutrennykh del SSSR), Obzor pechati, *Pogranichnik* (1946) 19–20, pp. 50–56; "Vyshe znamya ideynosti v literature (peredovaya), *Znamya* (1946) 10, pp. 27–37, and a sequel in the following issue (11–12), pp. 184–98; P. Afonin, "O tekh, kto zabyl traditsii Mayakovskogo," *Molodoy Bol'shevik* (1946) 7, pp. 42–47.

76. See Gleb Struve, "Anna Akhmatova," in Anna Akhmatova, *Sochinenia* I (Munich: Inter-Language Literary Associates, 1965), p. 10.

77. Harrison Salisbury, "Stalinist Jailing of Poet's Son Told," *New York Times,* Jan. 14 (1962).

78. See Amanda Haight, "Anna Akhmatova's *Poema bez geroya,"* *The Slavonic and East European Review,* XLV 105 (1967), p. 496.

79. A. A. Fadeev, "Iz perepiski," *Novy mir* 12 (1961), p. 195.

80. Two months after having written the letter Fadeev committed suicide. According to Mr. Salisbury, Moscow literary circles attributed the suicide to Fadeev's remorse over his role in the last years of Stalin, and his failure to support fellow artists when they fell into disfavor with the dictator.

81. Anna Akhmatova, *Stikhotvorenia* (Moscow: Goslitizdat, 1958), pp. 74–75.

82. Kruchenok, P. "Tri stikhotvorenia" (from Moldavian by Anna Akhmatova and M. Shekhter), *Oktyabr'* (1951) 2, pp. 5–8.

83. M. Makaryan. "Shest' stikhotvoreny" (from Armenian, Akhmatova et al.) *Novy mir* (1952) 3, pp. 66–71; L. Popov, "Tri stikhotvorenia (from Yakut, Akhmatova et al.) *Druzhba Narodov* (1953) 3, pp. 174–75; Li Bo [Li Po] "Stikhi iz kit. klassiki" (from Chinese, Akhmatova) *Ogonek* (1955) 23, p. 9. "Koreyskie stikhi, iz klassicheskoy poezii XV–XVI vv" (from Korean, Akhmatova) *Inostrannaya literatura* (1955) 2, p. 185.

84. A. Akhmatova, *Koreyskaya klassicheskaya poezia* (Moscow: Goslitizdat, 1956), p. 258.

85. A. Isaakian, "Stikhi" (from Armenian, Akhmatova et al.) *Druzhba narodov* (1956) 5, p. 71; M. Makarian, "Lyubov'" (Akhmatova et al.), *Ogonyok* (1956) 2, p. 24; P. Makrish, "Stikhi" (from Yiddish, Akhmatova et al.); *Druzhba narodov* (1956) 10, pp. 122–25; A. Toma, "Stikhi" (from Rumanian by Akhmatova et al.), *Inostrannaya literatura* (1956) 9, pp. 17–18.

86. Anna Akhmatova, "Petrograd 1916" and "Azia," *Literaturnaya Moskva* (1956) 1, pp. 537–539.

P. Antokolsky (ed.), *Den' Poezii* (Moscow: Moskovsky rabochy, 1956), p. 9. The selections in this work illustrate the relative freedom of the period;

it is significant that the editor had earlier been termed a "decadent, esthetizing" poet and had been condemned along with Akhmatova during the Zhdanov purge. See Victor Erlich, *Russian Formalism* (The Hague: Mouton, 1955), p. 122.

87. Fadeev, *loc. cit.,* p. 195.

88. A. Volkov, *Ocherki russkoy literatury kontsa XIX i nachala XX veka* (Moskow: Gosizdat, 1955), pp. 460–64 and A. Volkov, *Russkaya literatura XX veka* (Moscow: GosUchebPedizdat, 1957), p. 254, effectively illustrate the change; the first takes a direct Zhdanov view, and the second states that "during the Soviet period [Akhmatova, Gorodetsky, et al.] abandoned the esthetic principles of Acmeism which were alien to the new Soviet period."

89. A. V. Kulinin, *Ocherki po istorii russkoy sovetskoy poezii 20-x godov* (Kiev: Izd. Kievskogo Universiteta, 1958), p. 9.

90. Among the translations in the second half of the volume, there are a number which seem to have been selected by Akhmatova not only because of stylistic affinity, but also because they contain characteristic themes which would have been inadmissible in her original poetry during these years. (Soviet poets are usually provided by the publisher with intra-linear prose translations of poems in languages they do not speak; they may choose among them.) One hesitates to do Akhmatova the disservice of suggesting Aesopic intent when there was none, but some autobiographical parallels are too striking to ignore. Two poems from the Korean suggest such parallels (*Stikhotvorenia,* pp. 115, 118), and one could easily read another as a reference to Gumilyov's tragic death (p. 120). I talked to K. N. Grigoryan, an editor in the Pushkinsky Dom in Leningrad who worked closely with Akhmatova on translations from Armenian (they appeared in *Literaturnaya Armenia* (1959) 6, pp. 88–90, and in Grigoryan's edition of the poetry of Vaan Ter'yan (Moscow-Leningrad: Goslitizdat, 1950). Mr. Grigoryan said that although Akhmatova felt in principle that a poet should choose works for translation which were not consonant with his own moods, she did quite the opposite in practice. A summary of their discussion on this point was published by Mr. Grigoryan ("Za tochnost' i masterstvo poeticheskogo perevoda," *Literaturnaya Armenia* (1961) 3, pp. 84–85).

91. Anna Akhmatova, *"Slovo o Pushkine"* (k 125-letiyu so dnya smerti A. S. Pushkina), *Zvezda* (1962) 2, pp. 171–72.

92. Anna Akhmatova, "Dva Chetverostishia," *Novy mir* (1963) 1, p. 65.

93. The smuggled transcript of the trial is printed in full in the *New Leader* (1964) March, pp. 6–17. The twenty-four-year-old poet was arraigned under a law designed to prevent malingering, or "parasitism on society." The basis of the charge was that Brodsky was not engaged in "productive labor" in writing poetry, and the "proof" offered was that he had not been paid for it. Despite the active support of such respected

literary figures as Chukovsky and Marshak, testimony from other literary figures and scholars, and the fact that he had been paid for his translations from Polish and Serbian, he was found guilty and sentenced. The witnesses for the prosecution neither knew Brodsky prior to the trial, nor were they competent to judge his literary ability.

94. See Korney Chukovsky, "Chitaya Akhmatovu," *Moskva* (1964) 5, pp. 200–203. Chukovsky calls for a reevaluation of all Akhmatova's past work in the light of her recent major achievements. His comments on "Poema bez geroya" are most interesting, and explain some of the more obscure references in this extraordinary piece.

95. "Anna Akhmatova v Italii," *Posev,* December 18, 1964.

Chapter Two

1. This chapter appeared in a slightly different form as an article in the *Slavic and East European Journal,* XII, 2 (1968), pp. 141–56.

2. D. Maksimov, "Akhmatova o Bloke," *Zvezda* 12 (1967), p. 186.

3. A. Akhmatova, *loc. cit.,* "Korotko o sebe," p. 7.

4. Entry for October 26, 1911. *Dnevnik,* in *Sobranie sochineny* VII (Moscow-Leningrad: Goslitizdat, 1963), p. 76. Blok was himself, at the time of this entry, only thirty-one years old.

5. See Georgy Ivanov, *Peterburgskie zimy,* pp. 153ff.

6. *Tsekh poetov* is translated elsewhere as the "Poets' Guild," but since the word "guild" has lost in English its primary meaning of a union of craftsmen, this translation does not indicate Gumilyov's intent in choosing the name. Among the "charter members" of the Workshop were: Vladimir Narbut, whose work was considered exemplary by the Workshop; Count Komarovsky, a gentle, mentally unbalanced young poet whose poems were much admired by Gumilyov and Akhmatova; Mariya Moravskaya, a poet of some talent much influenced by Akhmatova; and Mikhail Zenkevich, who, since Akhmatova's death, is the last survivor of the original group. The Workshop included also a number of people not especially known for their poetry: Dmitry Kuzmin-Karavaev and his wife Elizaveta Yurevna, country neighbors and close personal friends of the Gumilyovs; M. L. Lozinsky, later renowned for his translation of Dante; Vladimir Pyast, a protegé of Blok; and Vasily Gippius, who in later years was to write the famous critical study of Gogol. Blok and Mikhail Kuzmin were briefly associated with the workshop at the beginning, and Georgy Ivanov, who left memoirs of these days, joined the group not long after.

7. *Istoki,* 1922. Partially quoted in Sergey Makovsky. *Na Parnase serebryannogo veka* (Munich: TSOP, 1963), p. 219.

8. *Dnevnik,* entry for January 12, 1913, p. 207.

9. *Dnevnik,* entry for December 17, 1912, p. 193.

10. A. Blok, "Bez bozhestva, bez vdokhnovenia," *Sochinenia* II (Moscow: Goslitizdat, 1955), pp. 361–370. It is interesting to note that Blok rejected the idea of Symbolism itself as a school, or any sort of formal union (see *Diary*, entry for April 17, 1912, p. 140).

11. Irina Odoevtseva, "Na beregakh Nevy," *Novy zhurnal* (1963), p. 76.

12. Maita Arnautová, "Akmeismus a 'nová vecnost,'" *Ceskoslovenská rusistika* IX, 1 (1964), p. 17.

13. K. Chukovsky, "Akhmatova i Mayakovsky," *Dom Iskusstv* 1 (1920), p. 23.

14. Osip Mandelshtam, "Utro akmeizma," *Sobranie Sochineny v dvukh tomakh* II (Munich: Inter-Language Literary Associates, 1966), pp. 362–67.

15. Valery Bryusov, "Novye techenia v russkoy poezii—Akmeizm," *Russkaya mysl'* (April 1913), pp. 134–42.

16. A. Blok, "Bez bozhestva . . .," p. 367.

17. Frank Reeve, *Aleksandr Blok: Between Image and Idea* (New York: Columbia University Press, 1962), pp. 202–203.

18. Valery Bryusov, "Novye techenia v russkoy poezii," *Russkaya mysl'* (April 1913), pp. 134–42.

19. Originally, the "Academy of Poetry." It was founded on the suggestion of Gumilyov, who enlisted Ivanov's help as director, and the close cooperation of such respected figures as N. V. Nedobrovo and V. A. Chudovsky.

20. "Zavety simvolizma," *Apollon* (May 1910), p. 20. Ivanov had read this address not only in Petersburg, but in Moscow the preceding March. The quotation which Ivanov uses here is from Pushkin's *Poet i tolpa*.

21. "O sovremennom sostoyanii russkogo simvolizma (po povodu doklada V. I. Ivanova)," *Apollon* (May 1910), pp. 21,30.

22. A. Blok, Bez bozhestva . . .," p. 365.

23. N. Gumilyov, "Pis'ma o russkoy poezii," *Apollon* 1 (1909), p. 22.

24. Petersburg, 1909–1917.

25. Later, the Makovskys became confidants of Akhmatova, and it was Makovsky who convinced Akhmatova to publish her poems in *Apollo*.

26. *Kniga otrazheny* I (Petersburg: Izd. Brat'ev Bashmakovykh, 1906).

27. Innokenty Annensky, "O sovremennom lirizme," *Apollon* 1, 2, 3 (1909).

28. *Stikhotvorenia*, p. 37.

29. *Ibid.*, p. 22.

30. "Traurny estetizm, I. F. Annensky—Kritik," *Apollon* 3 (1909), pp. 9–10.

31. For a detailed account of Annensky as poet and his relationship

to the contributors to *Apollon,* see Vsevolod Setchkarev, *Studies in the Life and Work of Innokenty Annensky* (The Hague: Mouton, 1963).

32. "O prekrasnoy yasnosti (zametki o proze)," *Apollon* (1910) 4, pp. 5–20.

33. The article referred to is Zhirmunsky's "Preodolevshie simvolizm," *Russkaya mysl'* 12 (1916), pp. 25–26.

34. See Boris Eikhenbaum, "O proze Kuzmina," *Skvoz' literaturu* (Leningrad: Akademiya, 1924), p. 197.

35. "Zhizn' stikha," *Apollon* 7 (1910, pp. 5–14; *"Poezia v Vesakh,"* *Apollon* 9 (1910), p. 42.

36. *Zolotoe Runo* 7–9 (1907), p. 32.

37. Quoted in Georgette Donchin, *The Influence of French Symbolism on Russian Poetry* (The Hague: Mouton, 1958), p. 77.

38. "Segodnyashny den' russkoy poezii," *Russkaya mysl'* 7 (1912), pp. 11–28.

39. "Heritage of Symbolism and Acmeism," *Apollon* 1 (1913), p. 42.

40. N. Gumilyov, *Pis'ma o russkoy poezii* (Petrograd: Mysl, 1923), p. 13. This book contains Gumilyov's essays and the "Letters on Russian Poetry" contributed to *Apollon.*

41. Osip Mandelshtam, "Utro akmeizma," *loc. cit.,* pp. 362–67.

42. Gorodetsky's article appeared after Gumilyov's in the same issue of *Apollon:* "Nekotorye techenia v sovremennoy russkoy poezii," p. 48.

43. *Portrety,* p. 241.

44. Gorodetsky's influence was a passing one. Never a first-rate poet, he seemed to attach himself to any current poetic movement; he had joined the "mystical anarchists," had written in the vaguest Symbolist manner, did a complete *volte-face* toward Russian folk poetry, and took part in the early stages of Acmeism. In any case, according to Mirsky, "by 1912 he had already outlived his talent."

45. Suzanne Bernard, *Le Poème en prose de Baudelaire jusqu'à nos jours* (Paris, Librairie Nizet: 1959), pp. 613, 610.

46. "A Stray Document," *Make It New: Essays by Ezra Pound* (London: Faber and Faber, 1934), p. 335. With regard to Pound's third point, Gumilyov had written in his article that the Acmeists "strove to break the bonds of meter by dropping syllables."

47. T. S. Eliot, "Hamlet and His Problems," *The Sacred Wood* (London: Methuen, 1920), p. 92. It is interesting to note that in 1921, the Russian critic Konstantin Mochulsky, analysed Akhmatova's poems in terms very similar to Eliot's objective correlative. "Poeticheskoe tvorchestvo Anny Akhmatovoy," *Russkaya mysl'* 3–4 (1921), p. 186.

48. See Victor Erlich, *Russian Formalism: History-Doctrine* (The Hague: Mouton, 1955), pp. 153–58.

49. Osip Mandelshtam, "Slovo i kul'tura," *Drakon* (Petersburg, 1921),

p. 77. This almanac was published by the Poets' Workshop, which had been revived by Gumilyov after the Revolution.

Chapter Three

1. "O stikhakh N. L'vovoy," *Russkaya mysl'* (1913) I, 1, p. 28. Nadezhda Lvova was a minor poet (whose name is remembered largely for the portrait of her by Serov), who committed suicide in 1913. Akhmatova's brief review of Lvova's *Staraya skazka* (Moscow: Altsiona, 1913) represents her only published critical remarks on modern poetry.

2. In *Evening,* one poem alone deals with a theme other than a woman's love (V Tsarskom Sele; Pushkin is the subject). In the much longer volume *Rosary* (some fifty-five poems), only four exclude the love theme.

3. In *The White Flock, The Plantain, At the Edge of the Sea* and *Anno Domini,* other themes predominate in only eight percent of the total; these are almost exclusively the art of poetry and Russia at war.

4. While the published material since that time is of course not representative, the theme occurs very frequently despite the restrictions. For example, see the selections in *Zvezda* 7 (1962), two poems from the cycle *Pesenki* and a long poem, "Melkhola," from *Obrazy iz drevnosti.*

5. Included in *Den' poezii* 1956, P. Antokolsky ed. (Moscow: Moskovsky rabochy, 1956).

6. Georgy Chulkov, "Anna Akhmatova," *Nashi sputniki 1912–1922* (Moscow: Izdanie Vasileva, 1922), p. 72.

7. Boris Eikhenbaum, "O sintaksise Anny Akhmatovoy," *Sovremennaya russkaya kritika* (Leningrad: Gosizdat, 1925), p. 213.

8. From a letter to Higginson, quoted in Charles Anderson, *Stairway to Surprise* (New York: Holt, 1960), p. 168.

9. Boris Eikhenbaum, *Anna Akhmatova, Opyt analiza* (Petersburg: Petropechat, 1923), p. 132.

10. V. Zhirmunsky, "Preodolevshie simvolizm," *Russkaya mysl'* 12 (1916), p. 33.

11. V. Zhirmunsky, *Kompozitsia liricheskikh stikhotvoreny* (Petersburg: OPOIAZ, 1921), p. 4. The word, "theme," when used at all, will be used only in the broadest and most general sense of a concept often repeated in Akhmatova's poetry. *Tema,* literally, "theme," is used by Zhirmunsky to designate the single occurrence of a concept which in recurrence is *motif.* The form *tema* will be used without translation in order to avoid the confusion which results from the many meanings of the English word.

12. (V 249). This poem, incidentally, was one of the earliest of Akhmatova's lyrics to receive broad distribution; it was printed in the *Apollo* and captured the imagination of the public. Later, it was set to music.

13. Ilya Ehrenburg, *Portrety russkikh poetov* (Berlin: Argonavty,

1922), p. 8. This article was written in 1919. The reference to the shawl here concerns a large shawl which Akhmatova affected; it became a kind of trademark.

14. Published for the first time in 1961. "Dva stikhotvoreniia iz pervoy tetradi," *Zvezda* 5, p. 146.

15. Other noteworthy examples of the treatment of love as pain and captivity occur typically in V 237, 245; Ch 174, 180, 204, 210; BS 102, 127, 149, 155, 170; P 73, 77, 85, 88; AD 39, 49. As illness and weariness: V 226, 234, 244; Ch 210; BS 106, 107, 108, 114, 123, 126, 132, 155; AD 53, 54.

16. This unusual device was much developed in later years; some of the most moving lines of *Requiem* derive their force from it. Often, there is the suggestion of a twin, or double, or mirror image—and in this, an interesting point of comparison with Blok.

17. For example, in the "Song of the Last Meeting," which is reproduced in Chapter I. Note that this poem makes use of the device just discussed, and that like the examples at hand, it is built on details of dress and the suggestion of an interior.

18. Only three such instances occur in the entire Chekhov Press edition. Similarly few are the instances when the gender of the speaker is indeterminate (e.g., descriptions of cities or tributes to other poets).

19. "Anna Akhmatova," *Russkaya mysl'* (July 1915), p. 55.

20. Mochulsky's formulation; "Anno Domini MCMXXI," *Sovremennye zapiski* 10 (1922), p. 385.

21. For example, V 232, 233; BS 152, 158; Ch 214.

22. Reserve, indifference and self-sufficiency are characteristic attributes of the lover as he often appears in Akhmatova's poems. His character is suggested in these epigrammatic lines: Kakuyu vlast' imeet chelovek/ Kotory dazhe nezhnosti ne prosit. ("What power has a man/Who does not even ask tenderness.") (Ch 187).

23. The imagery linking the heroine with a bird indicates the heroine as poet (BS 103, 199, 96; Ch 206, 195). The bird imprisoned or killed signifies inspiration forbidden or lost; often these poems seem to have an autobiographical reference to Gumilyov's objection to Akhmatova's writing.

24. Compare: Tikhy dom moy pust i neprivetliv/On na les glyadit odnim okom ("My silent house is empty and inhospitable; it looks onto the wood with one eye" Ch 198); Moy byvshy dom eshche sledil za mnoyu/Prishchurennym . . . okom ("My former home still followed me/With a squinting . . . eye.") From "Vrode monologa," 1942.

Chapter Four

1. K. Mochulsky, "Anna Akhmatova, Anno Domini MCMXXI," *Sovremennye zapiski* (1922) X, pp. 385–90. (Paris). Compare similar statements by Innokenty Oksenov (Review of the eighth edition of *Rosary*

and his review of *The Plantain,* both in *Kniga i revolyutsia* (1922) 7, p. 63 and (1921) 12, pp. 16–18; also S. Sumsky's review of *Anno Domini* in *Novaya russkaya kniga* (1922) 1, pp. 20–21.

2. Mikhail Pavlov, Reviews of *Anno Domini* and *At the Edge of the Sea, Kniga i revolyutsia* (1922), p. 72.

3. These poems were used in the rehabilitation of Akhmatova after the Zhdanovshchina; her attitude toward the emigration and toward connections with the West were cited by Fadeev in his appeal in behalf of her son Lev Gumilyov. The formula for the rehabilitation, which began slowly in 1958, is that "Akhmatova did not betray the motherland," meaning that she did not emigrate. See A. B. Kulinin, *Ocherki po istorii russkoy sovetskoy literatury 20–x godov* (Kiev: Izd. Kievskogo Universiteta, 1958).

4. If the main focus in the poem as a whole is the love motif, there is nevertheless here an inescapable suggestion of Pushkin's "Bronze Horseman." In the first part (of only eight lines), the famous statue is mentioned, and there is an evocation of Peter the Great. Interestingly, in connection with the Pushkin poem, there is the assumption that Peter the Great still lives—and that his horse strains "in menacing impatience." The love motif in the second part represents a kind of parallel with the second part of the Pushkin poem, and there is a return to the figure of Peter in the last stanza of Akhmatova's poem.

5. From "Prehistory," composed in 1945. *Stikhotvorenia* (1958), p. 82.

6. Composed in 1942. *Stikhotvorenia* (1958), p. 64.

7. "*Adolf* Benzhamena Konstana v tvorchestve Pushkina," *Vremennik Pushkinskoy Komissii* (Moscow-Leningrad: Akademia Nauk, 1936), pp. 91–114.

8. From "Slava tolpe," V. Bryusov, *Stikhotvorenia* (Minsk: Gosuchebpedizdat, 1955), p. 149.

9. Donchin, *op. cit.,* p. 161.

10. V. Zhirmunsky, "Preodolevshie simvolizm," *Russkaya mysl'* 12 (1916), p. 39.

11. It should be noted that in the 1958 edition of Akhmatova's poems, a surprisingly different variant of this poem appears on page 65. Although this version is dated 1944, and the date given for the one quoted above is 1946, the latter would seem to be the original. If it is a reworking, one wonders why Akhmatova did not use it for the 1958 edition; editorial pressure seems likely. In the version dated 1944, there is no suggestion of nostalgia for the past, and the petty details from a life remembered, which are so effective here between images suggesting the grandeur of the town, are not included. The reference to love is also absent. While the style remains intimate, the exclusion of these elements make a much less effective—and less characteristic—poem. In the poem from the 1958 collection, replacing *tsarskogo* with the word *drevnego*

makes little sense, since it does not continue the interesting pattern of accented and unaccented "a's."

12. Foreign cities, predictably, have a very small role in Akhmatova's poetry: Venice alone has an entire poem devoted to it; Paris is the setting for another. Nice and London are mentioned only once, each time in metaphors.

13. Leonid Grossman, "Anna Akhmatova," *Svitok* 4 (Moscow: Kooperativnoe izdatel'stvo pisateley, 1926), p. 305. It should perhaps be noted at this point that, as Grossman indicates, the images from rural Russia are employed to suggest the land as a whole; there is practically no "Nature description" per se in Akhmatova's poetry, which is oriented largely to the man-made world.

Chapter Five

1. Chudovsky, p. 25.

2. Yuly Aykhenvald, *Siluety russkikh pisateley* III (Berlin: Slovo, 1923), pp. 283–284.

3. See for example I 17; AD 58, 65; P 78; BS 108, 112, 153, 155, 166; Ch 181.

4. *Russkaya mysl'* (July 1915), p. 63.

5. Compare: Akh, pusty dorozhnye kotomki,/A na zavtra golod i nenast'e (V 245). Prophecy, foresight and presentiments represent a motif which suggests not only the powers ascribed to the suffering pilgrim in Russian tradition, but which also suggests the superstition that was so much a part of that tradition. O nyom gadala ya v kanun kreshchen'ya, Ya v yanvare byla ego podrugoy (V 230). Compare also V 242, V 224, BS 123, P 81, AD 61, BS 105, AD 53, I 27, 17, 4.

6. Chudovsky, p. 26.

7. Chudovsky, p. 24.

8. See for example Ch 201 (Ya u boga vymolyu proshchen'e,/I tebe i vsem kogo ty lyubish'—I shall ask forgiveness of God/For you and for all whom you love); Ch 211; BS 96, 132, 161, 170.

9. These two lines, which incidentally open the volume *The White Flock,* present an especial problem of translation, and a significant one with regard to the discussion here. "Pustynny" is not simply "empty" *(pustoy),* but carries the connotations: desert, uninhabited, wilderness. A "pustynnik" is an anchorite, a hermit who lives in the wilderness.

The use of the word "svetly" in Akhmatova's poetry is most unusual. In some instances, the ordinary meaning—light, bright, shining, radiant—is clearly intended. In others, the connotation is a negative one, not pleasant but sad, and seems to suggest a kind of emptiness. Davno Ya predchuvstvovala etot/svetly den' i opustely dom ("Long have I foreseen this/Bright day and abandoned house"); Po usopshemu svetlo gorevat' ("To grieve radiantly for the deceased"); Dolya materi svetlaya pytka ("The lot of a mother is a shining martyrdom"). With regard to the discussion in the text above, it is interesting to note that Akhmatova chose as an epigraph to *The White Flock* this line from Annensky: Goryu, i noch'yu doroga svetla ("I burn, and in the night the road is bright").

10. The same pattern, with variations, is used in V 234; Ch 181; BS 101, 152; AD 65.

11. Akhmatova simply calls Ivanov a liar, although much of what he has to say in *Peterburgskie zimy* occurs, in spirit at least, in other sources.

12. Georgy Ivanov, *Peterburgskie zimy*, p. 78. *Voz'mite, Khrista radi*— "Take it, for the sake of Christ"—is the formula for almsgiving.

13. V. A. Veselovsky, *Lyubovnaya lirika XVIII veka* (Petersburg: Tip. Yasnogorodskogo, 1909), pp. 37–38. Among many others, Veselovsky cites these examples: Voditsa kholodnyoshen'ka bezhala,/Devitsa edinyoshen'ka sidela ("The cold water was running by,/The maiden was sitting all alone"); Rechki kholodnye vodon'ki/Vy devushki posobite plakati ("The cold waters of the stream/You maidens help to weep.") The diminutives and archaisms cannot be rendered into English.

14. Veselovsky, *op. cit.*, *Lyubovnaya lirika . . .*, p. 44.

15. Nikolay Klyuev, *Polnoe sobranie sochineniy* I (New York: Chekhov Press, 1954), p. 195.

16. Quoted in A. Selivanovsky, *Ocherki po istorii sovetskoy poezii* (Moscow: Gosizdat, 1936), p. 48.

17. See Otsup's comments in *Izbrannoe*, pp. 29–30.

18. Both poets, for example, reworked Old Testament themes, Gumilyov in his earlier poetry, Akhmatova much later (e.g. Gumilyov's "The Prodigal" in *Chuzhoe nebo;* Akhmatova's "Lot's Wife" and "Rachel" composed after *Anno Domini*). In Gumilyov's *Kolchan*, the poem "Five-foot Iambs" tells of the desire to escape life after love lost, and to enter a monastery; it is in this regard parallel to Akhmatova's poem cited above. "The Cathedral at Padua" *(Kolchan)* depends on a juxtaposition of the sacred and the profane. One of Gumilyov's finest poems, "Heirs of Cain" *(Zhemchuga)*, suggests sincere religious reflection, and he doubts for the moment the superiority of the poet, of himself as a demigod and "porphyry idol among clay images." The theme of "The Gates of Paradise" is that the last shall be first: his vision of St. Peter is Akhmatova-like: I apostol Pyotr v dyryavom rubishche, slovno nishchiy, bleden i ubog. ("And Apostle Peter in a ragged, tattered garment, like a beggar, pale and poverty-stricken.")

19. Zhirmunsky, "Preodolevshie simvolizm," p. 39.

20. G. Lelevich, "Anna Akhmatova, Beglye zametki," *Na literaturnom postu*, Moscow, 1924. Parts of this essay are quoted in the *Literaturnaya entsiklopedia* article on Akhmatova.

21. Leon Trotsky, *Literatura i revolyutsia* (Moscow, Gosizdat, 1924), p. 33.

22. "Doklad Tovarishcha Zhdanova," p. 11.

23. Yuly Aikhenvald, *Poety i poetessy* (Moscow: Severnye Dni, 1922), p. 91.

24. Marc Slonim, *Modern Russian Literature: From Chekhov to the Present* (New York: Oxford, 1953), p. 220.

25. V. Chudovsky, "Poeticheskoe tvorchestvo Anny Akhmatovoy," *Russkaya mysl'* (March–April 1921), p. 186.

26. *Ibid*, p. 26.

27. Vladimir Nabokov, *Pnin* (New York: Doubleday, 1957), p. 56.

28. The hyphenated combinations, common in Russian folk poetry, do not translate into English.

29. Called Agrafena-kupal'nitsa, because it follows the Feast of St. John the Baptist (Ivan Kupalo), at midsummer. Significantly then, the contrast here is between love on midsummer's eve and abandonment the day following midsummer. The "frosty" cell suggests that the girl has been pining until the following autumn, when the action of the poem takes place.

30. Yury Tynyanov, *Arkhaisty i novatory* (Berlin: Priboy, 1929), pp. 550–51.

31. Boris Eikhenbaum, *Opyt analiza,* p. 120.

32. Leonid Grossman, "Anna Akhmatova," *Sbornik Svitok* 4 (Moscow: Kooperativnoe izdatestvo pisateley, 1926), p. 305.

Chapter Six

1. It would seem that a discussion of the interesting problem of Akhmatova's syntax might be included along with this topic. Boris Eikhenbaum, however, has treated it so exhaustively in his article "On the Syntax of Anna Akhmatova," and in his book, that these works must be considered definitive in this respect. Any abstraction or resumé would do these works an injustice, although passages relevant to the discussion of lexicon will be cited.

2. Aleksandr Blok, "Bez bozhestva, bez vdokhnovenia," *Sobranie Sochineny* II (Moscow: Goslitizdat 1955), p. 367.

3. V. Lvov-Rogachevsky, *Noveyshaya russkaya literatura* (Moscow: Frenkel, 1925), p. 281.

4. K. Mochulsky, Poeticheskoe tvorchestvo Anny Akhmatovoy," *Russkaya mysl'* (March–April 1921), p. 186.

5. "I cannot help ... complaining about human vocabulary ... I need to designate the secretive depths and implacable advance of that infinite host of beings, aspects, events, physical and moral tangles of horror and beauty—of that world, that undecipherable Other—with which ... the artist is faced; and I have no word for that except the poorest and tritest word of the human language; I shall say: the things of the world,

the *Things."* Jacques Maritain, *Poetry, Art and Things* (New York: Noonday, 1955), p. 1.

6. Some examples used in this section are from sources other than the five volumes used for analysis in the preceeding sections; a few are taken from poems written outside the time period fixed in the introduction. Page references are given only for those poems which are included in the five volumes. It was Mochulsky's article, cited above (fn. 4), which suggested the succeeding analysis of Akhmatova's weight-lightness opposition and, in part, her use of color.

7. This poem is included in the Gollerbakh collection, *Obraz Akhmatovoy.*

8. Viktor Vinogradov, *O poezii Anny Akhmatovoy* (Leningrad: Izdanie Foneticheskogo Instituta Yazykov, 1925), p. 59.

9. Compare this unusual use of whiteness with that of *svetly* (bright, radiant), discussed above. Annensky, parenthetically, speaks of death as *belaya radost' nebyt'ya* (the white joy of non-being).

10. For a detailed discussion of this convention in the two poets mentioned above, see R. Gustafson, "The Metaphor of the Seasons in *Eugene Onegin," Slavic and East European Journal* (1962) VI 1, pp. 6–20.

11. For other examples of winter as symbolic of happiness, see Ch 192, 200, 212, 216; BS 152; P 86.

12. There was a great interest in Japanese art during the decade in which Akhmatova began her career; comparisons of Akhmatova's lyrics with the delicacy and economy of Japanese art were inevitable (e.g., "Po povodu . . .," pp. 46 ff.). Eikhenbaum, however, rejected such comparisons on the basis that Japanese art was impressionistic, and he felt Akhmatova's economy of words to be a result of intensity of emotion rather than a striving for an impressionistic effect (*Opyt analiza,* p. 33). On the basis of color composition, however, the parallel does seem justified. Parenthetically, a further parallel to Annensky's use of color might be drawn here: he also often used one brilliant spot of color in the overall black and white scheme.

13. The color also occurs in more ordinary applications, e.g. Ch 200, BS 132, 163, P 83.

14. From the collection *Versty* (1922).

15. Similes introduced by *kak* seem to be avoided, although those introduced by *slovno* are more frequent. The preferred form for the simile is the instrumental case without preposition, often suggesting the folk manner.

Chapter Seven

1. E. Dobin, "Poezia Anny Akhmatovoy (Pervoe Desyatiletie)," *Russkaya literatura* 2 (1966), p. 155. N. V. Pervushin expresses himself

in a similar way: "There is no early Akhmatova. She was a mature poet from the beginning." ["O poezii Anny Akhmatovoy,"] *Russian Language Journal* XXI, 79 (June, 1967), pp. 8–14. Boris Filipoff, as quoted by Helen Muchnic, observed: "Akhmatova is fully and always Akhmatova, but Akhmatova of different ages—and for different ages." "Three Inner Emigrés: Anna Akhmatova, Osip Mandelshtam, Nikolay Zabolotsky," *The Russian Review* XXVI (January, 1967), p. 17.

2. Oddly enough, Akhmatova later separated this highly successful three-part poem into two independent ones, and incorporated the remaining part into the poem "Putyom vseya zemli."

3. That is, the authorized version, approved by Akhmatova in 1965, six months before her death. There are variants with more conventional endings. See Boris Filippov, *"Poema bez geroya"* Anny Akhmatovoy: zametki, *Vozdushnye puti* II (New York: Grynberg, 1961), pp. 177–78. Another variant is given in the same volume (footnote on p. 15).

4. "Poema bez geroya," *Vozdushnye Puti* II (New York: Grynberg, 1961), p. 116.

5. *Ibid.,* p. 113.

6. Korney Chukovsky, Chitaya Akhmatovu," *Moskva* 5 (1964), pp. 200–203.

7. "Anna Akhmatova's *Poema bez geroya,"* *The Slavonic and East European Review* (July 1967), pp. 474–96.

8. Anna Akhmatova, "Vospominania ob Al. Bloke," *Zvezda* 12 (1967), p. 186.

9. "Iz pis'ma k N.," *Vozdushnye Puti* II (New York: Grynberg, 1961), p. 113.

10. E. Dobin, *Poezia Anny Akhmatovoy* (Leningrad: Sovetsky pisatel', 1968), p. 245.

11. "Iz pis'ma k N.," p. 113.

12. See Akhmatova's poem, "The Voice of Memory" (Golos pamyati), written in 1913 and dedicated to O.A. Glebova-Sudeykina.

13. Boris Filippov, *"Poema bez geroya* Anny Akhmatovoy: zametki," *Vozdushnye puti* II (New York: Grynberg, 1961), pp. 169–70.

14. *Poema bez geroya,* Amanda Haight, ed. Footnote to p. 491.

15. A. S. Pushkin, *Polnoe Sobranie Sochineny,* vol. II (Moscow: Akademiya nauk, 1956), pp. 196–97.

16. For variant readings of the ending, see note 3, above.

17. Georg von Rauch, *History of Soviet Russia.* New York: Praeger (1967), p. 242.

18. The close juxtaposition of gutturals suggests a throat constricted by grief. Akhmatova consciously used juxtapositions of glottal stops for emotional signification; elsewhere she notes the use of juxtaposed "k"s to suggest extreme agitation. The vowel sounds are carefully ordered in a progression from front to back. The line descends in intonation as in

physical articulation. The following line, as characteristic of Akhmatova's earlier orchestrations, reverses the procedure.

19. The Feast of the Protection of the Mother of God, which is little known in the West, is an important Orthodox festival, commemorating her appearance in Constantinople in the Tenth Century. Kneeling in tears in the center of a church, she extended her veil over all the people, who felt the grace of her protection. See Leonid Ouspensky and Vladimir Lossky, *The Meaning of Icons*. Boston: Book and Art Shop (1952), pp. 153–54.

Conclusion

1. Georgy Adamovich, "Moi vstrechi s Akhmatovoy," *Vozdushnye puti* V, p. 112.

Selected Bibliography

1. WORKS
   ANNA
   AKHMATOVA, *Stikhotvorenia*. Petersburg: Petropolis-Alkonost, 1923. *Izbrannye stikhotvorenia*. New York: Chekhov, 1952.
   Stikhotvorenia. Moscow: Goslitizdat-Khudozhlit, 1958.
   Stikhotvorenia (1909–1960). Moscow: Goslitizdat-Khudozhlit, 1961.
   Beg vremeni. Moscow-Leningrad: Sovetsky pisatel', 1965.
   Sochinenia. Munich: Inter-Language Literary Associates, 1965.

2. BIOGRAPHY
   There is as yet no biography of Akhmatova. Most of the biographical sources available were rejected by Akhmatova during her lifetime. Akhmatova's autobiographical notes are few, and usually focus on others: Bloc, Modigliani, Mandelshtam. The best source of biographical information is: Dobin, E. *Poezia Anny Akhmatovoy*. Leningrad: Sovetsky pisatel', 1968. The information here is sparse, but reliable.

3. LITERARY STUDIES
   ARVATOV, V. "Grazhdanka Akhmatova i tovarishch Kollontay," *Molodaya Gvardia*, 5–5 (1923), 141–51. Interesting as the first example of the "Party-line" type of criticism. It is written on a pitifully low critical level.
   BLOK, ALEKSANDR: "Bez bozhestva, bez vdokhnovenia," *Sobranie sochineny* II. Moscow, 1955. 361–370. Blok's poor opinion of Acmeism and words of praise for Akhmatova.
   BRYUSOV, V. "Segodnyashny den' russkoy poezii," *Russkaya mysl* VII (1912) II–28. An early and thoughtful reaction to Akhmatova's first volume.
   "Novye techenia v russkoy poezii—Akmeizm," *Russkaya mysl'*, 4 (1913), 134–92.
   CHUDOVSKY, V. "Poeticheskoe tvorchestvo Anny Akhmatovoy," *Russkaya mysl'* (March–April 1921) 186–91. One of the first attempts at critical analysis; contains useful insights.

CHUKOVSKY, K. "Akhmatova i Mayakovsky," *Dom iskusstv* I (1920) 23–42. Literary disputes of the twenties.

"Chitaya Akhmatovu," Moskva 5 (1964) 200–203. Very helpful in interpreting the references in *The Poem Without a Hero*.

DOBIN, E. *Poezia Anny Akhmatovoy.* Leningrad: *Sovetsky pisatel'*, 1968. An excellent, sensitive study, informed by the author's acquaintanceship with Akhmatova, but rather weak on the later period.

EIKHENBAUM, BORIS. *Anna Akhmatova. Opyt Analiza.* Petersburg: Petropechat', 1923. The standard work on the early period. Despite its approach to Akhmatova's poetry through Acmeist theory, it is still quite useful.

GROSSMAN, LEONID. "Anna Akhmatova," *Sbornik Svitok* IV (1926) 295–305. Sometimes impressionistic, but thoroughly perceptive; an appreciation of Akhmatova.

MOCHULSKY, K. "Poeticheskoe tvorchestvo Anny Akhmatovoy," *Russkaya mysl'* (March–April 1921), 186–94. An interesting experiment in criticism; physio-psychological reaction to Akhmatova's poetry.

PAVLOVSKY, A: *Anna Akhmatova: Ocherk tvorchestva.* Leningrad: Lenizdat, 1966. First detailed study since the 1920's. Draws on earlier critical essays, avoids problems that might be troublesome for a Soviet critic, but on the whole worthwhile.

VINOGRADOV, V. *O poezii Anny Akhmatovoy.* Leningrad: Trudy foneticheskogo instituta, 1925. Linguistic approach; in part, a polemics with Eikhenbaum.

ZHIRMUNSKY, V. "Preodolevshie simvolizm," *Russkaya mysl'* 12 (1916), 25–26.

4. RELATED WORKS

Doklad Tovarishcha Zhdanova o zhurnalakh *Zvezda i Leningrad, Sovetskaya kniga* 8–9 (1946).

GOLLERBAKH, ERIKH. *Obraz Akhmatovoy:* Antologia Leningrad: 1925. Poems written to Akhmatova by contemporaries.

GORODETSKY, S. "Nekotorye techenia v sovremennoy russkoy poezii," *Apollon* 1 (1913), 46–50. Gorodetsky's part of the Acmeist "manifesto."

GUMILYOV, N. "Zavety simvolizma i akmeizm," *Apollon* 1 (1913), 42–45. Gumilyov's part of the Acmeist "manifesto."

5. TRANSLATIONS

The best translations of Akhmatova into English are some twenty-six poems in *Modern Russian Poetry,* ed. Vladimir Markov and Merrill Sparks (New York: Bobbs Merrill, 1967).

Index